Meditation

A WAY TO TAKE CHARGE OF YOUR LIFE

by
Arun "Yogi" Parekh M.A.

The more you know about yourself,
the more you empower yourself.

ISBN 0-9723574-0-8

Designed by
Nandan V. Nagwekar of
NVN Advertising, Mumbai, (India)
Email : nandanvn@vsnl.com

Printed by
Anjan S. Lalaji
Aim Printers
R-10/2, Bangur Nagar, Goregaon (W),
Mumbai – 400 090. (India)
Phone : 0091-22-8735579

September 2002

Published by
Arti Integrated Training
6921 Spur Road,
Springfield, Va. 22153 (U.S.A.)
Phone: (703) 644-9011
www. ArtiPresentations.com

Publisher Declares

If this book fails to meet your expectations
at all, you may return it to us. We shall
gladly refund the full price of it.

Dedicated with love
to my wife
Bharti
for helping me
discover my passion

FOREWARD

This book is a result of numerous inquiries from my students, seminar participants and audience members of my public lectures. I found them looking for such a book on meditation that may cover the following elements: (1) meditation explained in a layman's level of understanding, (2) a discussion of different methods to suit different minds, (3) easy-to-follow steps to meditate, without much altering their accustomed lifestyles, (4) author's personal testimonies, and (5) benefits of the practice, focusing mainly on their career-life relationships. **Thus emerged this book**.

It doesn't matter whether or not you are experienced in meditation. This book will add to your journey, heighten your awareness, and enhance your philosophical perception, enabling you now to respond to the same events of your daily life with more poise and awareness. You also will feel encouraged to realize, within you, the presence of an infinite source of wisdom, guidance and foreknowledge of the upcoming events in your life, helping you alter your belief system—a key to empowering ourselves over the stress, indecisiveness and restlessness in our lives.

Uncommon to most books on this subject, I have included two chapters, "The Seven Important Tips" and "The Living Meditation," both with several personal examples, encouraging you to enjoy the best results of your practice. The former needs no explanation; its very title is self-explanatory. The latter presents three powers, the Power of Reminder, the Power of Environment and the Power of Visualization, the knowledge of which we possess already, but is often forgotten or under utilized. This chapter will remind you of these powers within you and help you lead your journey to a higher level and take greater charge of you life.

The last section on "Meditation And Stress" discusses how an altered perception can more empower you over what is unchangeable in our lives. It is my belief that our heightened philosophical perception is the only effective way to better manage the rising stress, balance career-life relationships, enhance our own personal evolution and deal with the challenges of uncertainties in our lives. **The Buddha and Christ** met the challenges and tribulations in their lives far greater than we normally face today, and yet they lived more fully than us. Our level of mental perception is everything in our lives.

This book is about various methods of meditation, their benefits in our different realms of life, and my personal journey. It is divided into three sections, the concept, methods and benefits of meditation, and each section further into its relevant chapters. Each chapter opens with a quote, and closes with a brief topic summary and chapter highlights, reinforcing the message of the chapter. In order to maximize your practice, I recommend that you first read this book completely before you begin practicing your meditation.

I possess an undergraduate degree in Philosophy from University of Bombay, and a graduate degree, with honors, in Transpersonal Studies, from Atlantic University, Virginia Beach. I am an earnest student of comparative religions and human consciousness. My philosophical and spiritual inquiries began from the early years of my life, and gradually developed into an irresistible urge to seek their answers. This journey of self-discovery led me to *Autobiography of A Yogi* by Paramahansa Yogananda. I found many of my life enigmas explained in his writings and my meditative practice.

Regardless of your personal faith, convictions, and level of interest in meditation, you will find this book informative, thought provoking and inspiring. If you believe in the power of your mind over your body, and are not making enough progress, this simple mental discipline, meditation, will help you realize many possibilities of your life. I have no doubt that this book charged with numerous personal experiences will find one day a niche of its own, largely in the hearts of those who are seeking better ways of living--living with greater self-dignity, independence and a purpose everyday.

In a final word, I would like to share a **personal anecdote**. In one of my recent seminars of Meditation and Stress Management, I asked the participants as my usual practice: What had brought them to my seminar and what precisely they would like to take home. Nicole, a pharmacist in a local hospital, had this to respond, "Nothing in particular. While going through your advertised material, I simply *felt drawn* to discover more about the subject and I decided at once to register." I asked no more to Nicole. Similar were the responses of Robert, a podiatrist, Charles McCall, a retired Navy captain, Dave Pond, an airline pilot, and many more, in several of my past presentations.

It will not surprise me therefore, if you experience too, a sense of *felt drawn* while reading this book. Some psychic energy flowing in nature attracts minds invariably, living in the same level of frequency, no matter how apart physically. Should you ever *feel drawn* to share or discuss with me about the subject matter of this book, I will be happy to respond.

Please do not dismiss this book after turning few pages, and not even after its first reading. I urge you to save it. One day, at some point in your life's journey, you may find it handy and beneficial evermore. Far more than the worldly favors, **my primary interest in writing** this book is only to reach out to those seeking guidance and encouragement in their journey of personal growth and development but do not know how to begin and where to turn for further help. This book possesses the potential to unlock many possibilities in your life.

I wish you the best.

Arun "Yogi" Parekh, M.A.
(Speaker, Trainer, Author)
Email: Yogi@ArtiPresentations.com
www: ArtiPresentations.com

September 2002

ACKNOWLEDGEMENTS
How May I Thank You?!

From the time I began working on this book, I realized that an undertaking of some serious writing, particularly the one intended to connect with readers through personal experiences, summons forth a resolve and commitment exceeding the one normally exercised in everyday life. This applies more to the people like me, who are not articulate in writing to the level of speaking, and at the same time, not ready by nature, to have a ghostwriter between them and their readers. At the end of meeting the varied challenges today, however, my joy surmounts all moments of pains and frustration experienced during this process over the last three years.

I am indebted first to my three daughters and their husbands, Heena-Ashish, Reeta-Bijal, and Priya-Faisal for their unconditional support to my work and growth, at all times, in whatever way they could, and at times, by going even out of their ways.

I was clearly aware from the beginning that I had something to offer to others, touching their hearts and souls, and improving their overall quality of life. I was therefore looking for such people to join this crusade of mine who may not be editors professionally, but can closely connect to my thoughts and vision, and help me effectively deliver my message. I must admit that I was fortunate to have Reeta, Faisal and Christian to assist me in my endeavor.

They came from different backgrounds, education, culture and faiths. Each edited, examined and presented their points of view, differently and yet supplementary to others', offering the book a deeper meaning and insight.

Christian, my ex-colleague and a friend, was kind of god-sent and joined our team lately, but caught up with us. Thank you, Christian, for spending many evenings in editing, offering me detailed reasoning behind those edits and suggestions, and happily undertaking the review of the final version of the manuscript.

Faisal brought grammatical clarity, logic and an added point of view to the writing. I cannot thank you enough, Faisal, for your valued suggestions offered in different areas of the making of this book, and staying committed to editing and timely returning the material against your increasing responsibilities at your work.

Without Reeta's help, my vision would not materialize so soon. At one stage when I was about to drop this arduous project, she motivated me *to arise and move on.* The book has passed through several versions of editing, and rewriting over with which Reeta has remained involved throughout. Thank you, Reeta, for helping make this process as my journey, a success and a heck of an experience. Thanks so much to Bijal for his forbearing inconveniences on several occasions, especially during the last few months, and thus offering his support to this work.

My thanks to Heena for her faith in my abilities and taking time to periodically remind me that *I can do it,* and to Ashish for his continual support, and in-depth analysis of my writings whenever taken to him. Thank you, Priya for spending many long hours, though tired at times after your college and work, to proofread and edit the initial writings of this book, and lately transporting its chapters back and forth, between Faisal and me.

I am also thankful to Mridula Vyas and Kathie Scriven,

both professional editors, for rendering their skills to early writings of this book, to Bhavin Shah for his encouraging words and valued suggestions, to Pankajbhai Shah for the final proof reading with a sense of priority, to Chetan Lalaji for helping place this book in a final shape, and to Nandan Nagwekar for his untiring efforts in creating the cover design.

In a sense, this book is co-authored by all those whose names are dearly mentioned herein; my name stands out in this book only as responsible for the inaccuracies and imperfection, if any, overlooked in it.

Above all, my deepest gratitude to Bharti, my truly better half, without whose support it would not be possible for me to pursue my passion as a full time pursuit, and encouraging me *to move on* through her taking pride and delight in my progress.

Finally, my sincere thanks to Anjan Lalaji of AIM Printing to accommodate my printing needs, and timely completing them with quality and smiles always.

September 16, 2002

ABOUT THE AUTHOR

Mr. Parekh, a graduate in Philoshphy from Atlantic University, Virginia Beach, Va, is a speaker with intrnational repute, seminar leader, college teacher and president of his speaking-&-training company.

He believes that developing our philosophical perception is an effective way to knowing ourselves better, recognizing further possibilities of our lives, playing well our diverse roles, and bringing a balance in our work-life relationship.

"My life's only mission is to reaching out to others, helping them recognize their power of inner silence, which meditation promises," Yogi declares. Not until we learn to successfully communicate with ourselves for a few minutes daily, regardless of the nature of the discipline used, we cannot reach the position of making better judgements, sustaining a positive attitude, developing immunity against the rising stress, and truly appreciating what we possess in material achievement and relationship.

TABLE OF CONTENTS

SECTION I

Concept, Purpose, and Tips

Chapter 1
MEDITATION :
A Way to Take Charge of Your Life

Chapter 2
MEDITATIVE VISUALIZATION

Chapter 3
THE SEVEN IMPORTANT TIPS

MEDITATION
A Way To Take Charge Of Your Life

*"All man's most miseries derive from his not being
able to sit quietly for few minutes in a room alone."*
(Blaisal Pascal)

Our life in the West, particularly in the United States
has phenomenally changed since World War II.
Our outward appearance and material pursuits have
become a driving force of our living, sometimes even at
the cost of meeting the needs of our health and
obligations to our families. We have grown as the
strongest nation, putting together the disciplined armies
and navies, sophisticated weapons and missiles,
agricultural and industrial developments, and space
and electronic technologies. We have made an enormous
progress on the waters, lands and in the outer space.
All these achievements have placed us in a position
exemplary to other nations. This progress, however,
seems to have heavily cost us in other areas.

Our Rising Time-Urgency

In our drive for material pursuits, we have
overlooked the needs of other areas in our lives, equally
important, to make our lives overall happy and
complete. By over extending ourselves in only one
direction, making ourselves materially happier, and not

taking time out to enough relax ourselves and duly meeting our obligations to our families, we have invited, often unknowingly, other undesirable elements into our lives. These include: the rising of unmanageable stress and its adverse effects such as health and mental disorders, splits in families, decline in family values and boredom in life.

The more we have grown modernized, the more we have lost peace in our lives. The more we have advanced in science and technologies, the more we have lost connection with ourselves. The more we have endeavored to touch the distant planets, the more we have lost touch with our own. The more we have marched together as a nation to reach the highest peak of power and affluence, the farther we have left behind our individuality. The more we have searched for success outside us, the more we have lost harmony within us. **George Carlin** expresses the same in different words, "We have learned how to make a living, but not a life; added years to our life, but not life to our years." It is high time that we reexamine our priorities and the direction of our progress.

Why Meditation?

You might have experienced, at one time or another, that when deeply preoccupied with a problem, the solution of it seems to be moving farther from our sight. But when we take our mind away from it for a while, the solution emerges mysteriously. This problem could be solving a mathematical equation, finding a right word or thought while editing a piece of writing, troubleshooting an error at work or seeking a solution in a real life predicament. As a good night's sleep heals fatigue of our body and rejuvenates our brain cells for another long day, shifting our mind to a relaxed state temporarily renders a new perception to the troubling situation and opens up a new possibility.

A biographical study of spiritual masters and great thinkers will reveal that **a realization of some profound experience or thought has occurred to them only when they were in their mental solitude,** a voluntary seclusion—a home away from their own. When we train our mind to relax daily, withdrawing it from its relentless thought processes and daily pressing demands, we begin experiencing the presence of our higher consciousness within us, an infinite source of our guidance and potentials, which otherwise remain unrecognized all our life.

This training of shifting our mind's focus to the state of deepest relaxation possible, for a few minutes daily, is called meditation. In meditation, we shift our focus, not on a different activity, but on calming our thoughts and emotions. This altered focus helps us to better perceive our daily priorities and life's overall progress. It is a technique to regain our inner harmony through rising above the troubling thoughts, often related to the unpleasant experiences of our past such as failures, regrets, traumas, guilt, and fears; and the anxieties of future.

For the lasting success in the area of our self-improvement, changes must take place from within us; not in our outer behaviors only. The external modification does not promise a long term result. Practicing meditation alters us inside out. Though this process is slow and demands enormous amount of patience, it promises a lasting success, making us better human beings and proud of ourselves evermore. It alters us inside subtly and effortlessly, like a fruit naturally emerging from its flower. With the growing self-awareness in regular practice of meditation, our perception to human life elevates, and with that transforms our attitude to our relationships with the world and its events in our day-to-day life.

Though still juggling with the myriad responsibilities in our daily life, same as before, such as dealing with commute, travels, work, relationships and health, we now respond to them differently, with more poise and awareness. We grow more conscious of the consequences of our acts and the purpose of our lives. We do not react as mechanically and impulsively as before. Meditation is a way to enjoy each of the cardinal aspects of our life to its fullest—health, personal relationship and worldly success.

The deepening level of silence, with our growing practice of meditation, leads our mind higher from its attachment of our day-to-day world. This places our mind in a better position to examine our thoughts, phobias and mental proclivities, and understand the deep-rooted unpleasant memories of our past. It helps us to be non-reactionary and non-judgmental in our attitudes. It helps develop our philosophical awareness to better adapt ourselves to what is unchangeable, to accept the unpredictable, and discover ways to turn impediments into our personal growth.

Regardless of the varied names given to it by different faiths, the only purpose of meditation is to calm our ever-turbulent mind so that we may develop a better perception of the circumstances, relationships and events in our lives at a given moment. Meditation brings more clarity in our thinking, poise in our conduct and prudence in our decisions.

We all generally seek unconditional love in our relationships, eternal happiness in our material possessions, and lasting gratification in fulfillment of our desires. But our day-to-day experiences seem to be proving often otherwise; all those things wherein we see joy, love and happiness seem to be bringing us frustration and miseries instead. We seldom realize that the cause of our suffering lies in our misidentification, and erroneous notion of success. Meditation brings us a sense of compromise with the transitory nature of the world we live in, and what we receive in response to our expectations from it.

We little realize that relationship is often a result of our mutual convenience, and that our transitory natured material possessions cannot promise lasting happiness. Our expectations of happiness in the earthly relationships and worldly achievements often prove disappointing to us. Practicing meditation helps us develop our discriminatory sense, an insight to distinguish between right and wrong, real and illusory.

Another area that seems to be bringing us disappointment and unhappiness is our tendency to compare ourselves with others. We normally judge our level of success through the sight of others. There is no yardstick as such that determines an ideal level of success in one's life. There is no such scale that determines a precise amount of happiness one must have to be happy.

You alone know how successful or happy you are. You are the best judge of the direction and progress of your life, and the level of success and happiness in your life. Meditation helps us know better about ourselves. The more we know about ourselves, the more we feel truly proud of ourselves, making us rise above our competitive comparison. We do not need then to show off others how successful and happy we are. We are in harmony with ourselves and content within with our material possessions. Meditation helps us someday realize this state in our lives. I have discussed about this in length in the last Section of this book.

Meditation is a way to rightly balance our priorities at every stage of our lives. **Maharshi Mahesh Yogi,** the founder of the Transcendental Meditation, once declared that meditation if practiced by even one percent of the population of America, it would generate a positive change in the overall thinking of the entire nation.

A Way in the East

The only purpose of meditation in the East is to find God in life. It is a way to creating a bridge between us and our Creator. **Paramahansa Yogananda** called it "the science of God-realization," or "God-commune," a legacy of the East from the time unknown. The ultimate purpose of meditation, according to the Hindus and Buddhists, is to attain the awareness of God in our daily life—the eternal quest of every human soul. That is why meditation is commonly referred to by these faiths as a spiritual practice, a practice that awakens our divine spark within us and helps us speed our spiritual evolution, the purpose of our life's journey.

In the *Yoga Sutra* by sage Patanjali over two thousand years ago, meditation is discussed at a great length. The word "yoga" in Sanskrit means a union, the union of the finite with the infinite, of an individual soul with the Spirit. Meditation is one of the eight-fold steps in the Patanjali's classic. Physical aerobics, moral disciplines, breathing, postures, etc. are the other topics in this book geared to having a sound health and ability to hold concentration longer to prepare students for meditation, an advanced step of the yoga.

In those times, prior to the beginning of the conventional way of schooling, the young boys in the East would spend most of their time, in the fellowship of their teachers and study the science of yoga to attain a good health and balanced living thorough developing the qualities such as of concentration, persistence, forbearance, and discrimination between right and wrong. Though the emphasis of teaching used to be on developing noble human qualities at early age, the teacher also would teach other subjects such as astronomy, astrology, health, philosophy and mathematics. This would bring in students a balance of learning of both worlds, inner as well as outer. When the age is young, the body and mind can be trained more easily than the later age, which helps a longer duration of meditation.

Though largely a psychological discipline to voluntarily rise above our mind's untiring thought processes, the benefits of meditation cannot be fully attained until one develops, through various disciplines of yoga, the sustained physical postures, a heightened sense of positive attitude toward both self and others, and deepest level of concentration possible. Meditation is therefore one of the eight-fold steps of yoga according to Patanjali. A teacher would modify the practice of meditation according to his students' psychophysical make up, mental proclivities and the level of spiritual orientation developed.

In the ancient times, the common practice of communicating at an individual level with God was meditation, a way of silent commune through holding the mind's focus at the center between the closed eyes. Meditating becomes easier and more effective when done in a quiet place, away from noise and other distractions. **The Bible** has the same reference: When you pray, enter into your closet...and your Father who sees in secret shall reward you openly. (Matthew 6:6) The more we have privacy, the easier we can hold our focus. The more we have solitude, the more we are immune to the influences of the external distractions. The more tranquil we are within, the more aptly we are to experience the presence of our higher self.

I have discussed here this timeless method of meditation, presenting it the way I have best understood and realized in my own life. In this book, I have however altered the focus of meditation, from god-commune as common, the objective of the practice in the East, to attaining the state of mental relaxation. In our fast-paced life, we seldom find the occasions of true relaxation compared to anything else in life. We all realize, at one time or another, that we need to slow down a little in the interest of our physical health and mental peace, and yet we are not ready to sacrifice our march for material pursuits even an inch. I believe that meditation can be an effective solution to our way of living.

In this book, I have submitted to you four methods of meditation, each of which I have personally experimented individually as well as in combination with another, to suit different minds and life styles. These techniques are simple to follow. Choose the one that suits you the best and practice it for a few weeks sincerely before switching to another. Unavailability of time should not be an excuse for a progressive mind. A wise person is the one who is ready to drop a dime for a quarter.

This seemingly small discipline of meditation has enormous power to transform our lives. If practiced regularly, it will impact positively every sphere of our lives, enabling us to enjoy our health, work, and relationships evermore, and bringing more of a balance between our work and life, the most needed element for our healthy living in our present fast-paced living. I wish to reinstate here the **Pascal**'s observation: "All man's most miseries derive from his not being able to sit quietly for few minutes in a room alone."

The Three Benefits I Most Enjoy

Though the most of the last section of this book is dedicated to the benefits of meditation in different realms of our lives, I wish to briefly share with you a few examples of how meditation has profoundly influenced my life. Reading about an abstract topic like meditation could be a lifeless task. The highest interest of every reader is to finding out how a particular book may best improve his or her quality of life. I have therefore added here the three major benefits that I have continued enjoying for years in diverse areas of my life.

(1) Heightened Self-Awareness: Meditation develops a sense of self-awareness in us, a better sense of awareness not only about our acts and behaviors, but about our motives and thoughts. It checks our tendency to normally acting mechanically and impulsively. It makes us more thoughtful of our behaviors before they are demonstrated.

If we condense all teachings of the Buddha into few words, the word *"jagrati,"* meaning self-awareness will stand out in them. In all his teaching, he stressed on acting with awareness. He strongly discouraged his disciples behaving impulsively, absent-mindedly or mechanically. The Buddha contended that we end up, at times, in a state of remorse and self-condemnation particularly because we allowed our conduct governed by our unchecked thoughts and feelings. All our violent acts are forced by our ungoverned emotions such as anger, greed, jealousy and vengeance.

Walking with eyes closed invites falls. When aware of the consequences of our act at a particular point of time, we may restrain from doing it. I was once seized by anger, considered to be a powerful foe of our growth in any realm. Raising my self-awareness in meditation helped me discover that I was on a wrong path. I have shown in length later how I could overcome my temperamental frailty by the very practice of meditation.

I get angry even today, but not to the extent and frequency as I used to. Furthermore, I can now foresee my anger emerging, which helps me prepare myself to diffuse its energy by quickly altering the state of my mind. Those with a high a sense of self-awareness are often found, compared to others, more composed in their temperament, careful in making decisions, thoughtful in dealing with others, and ready to accept accountability for their actions.

(2) *Better Prioritized Daily Demands:* Meditation benefits us in perceiving and effectively prioritizing our lives' daily demands. We saw earlier that meditation is a technique to calm our turbulent thoughts and chaotic emotions during our practice. This sense of clarity in our perception helps us to better view the events and our commitments in our personal lives. The following illustration may offer you a better understanding of what I intend to convey here.

According to an internet source, while speaking about the work-life relationship to a university audience some years ago, **Brian Dyson, CEO** of Coca Cola Enterprise compared our position in our day-to-day life with that of a juggler. He said that imagine your life as a game in which we are juggling some five balls in the air. You name them—work, family, health, friends and spirit—and we are trying to keep all of them in the air. You will soon discover that the work is a rubber ball, which if dropped, bounces back. But the other four balls are made of glass. If you drop any of them, they will be irrevocably scuffed, marked, damaged or even shattered. They will never be the same. You must understand that and strive for the balance in your life.

Meditation promotes temperamental balance and clarity of thinking in us, helping us to view our daily priorities from a higher plateau. The longer and deeper we tune with our inner silence, beyond our clamorous mind, the better we are in a position to perceive our relationships with our demands and commitments.

When confronted by countless priorities, each seems to be claiming the same level of our importance. In a situation like this, it is not our thinking or intellect, but only our developed insight rescues us. Real life scenarios are often too complicated to find answers for in the books on self-help. Based on my personal experience on several occasions, it is equally true that our life's enigmas have to be solved by ourselves; no one else can be of much help in it. It is such a situation in one's life when one is all alone to face, struggle and resolve.

Certain paradoxes in our lives must be solved only by the one who claims it as "my life," and no one else. Developed perception in the silence of meditation is our rescuer in the events when we are faced by our life's enigmas and conflicting priorities. Call this heightened sense of perception, wisdom, insight, prudence or intuitive feeling; all mean the same, and it cannot be learned in classrooms of conventional schools, universities or seminars. It comes only through our self-realization and self-endeavors.

(3) *Increased Immunity Over Hostile Encounters:* The area in my personal life where meditation has most benefited me is that of my inter-personal relationships. It has helped me develop personal indifference towards the unfriendly behaviors and inappropriate comments of others.

Encountering inimical encounters, no matter where we are—in relationships, commutes, travels, workplaces, shopping malls, or social gatherings—is generally our common experience. You might have occasionally asked yourself: "How can I deal with this unpleasant reality of almost everyday, at work or home, without losing the sanity of my mind?" "How can I handle this day-to-day uncomfortable encounter without further aggravating the situation?" "How can I retain my self-control in this turbulent relationship?"

In one period of my life, I had similar questions for myself. I did not have any answers then but to quietly endure them myself. Meditative discipline immensely helped me, not only in better understanding the adverse situations, but also in training my mental attitude, making those things more tolerable.

I have realized that duality is the very nature of the world we live in. The good and evil, just and unjust, love and hate are the inseparable parts of our environment, and their very coexistence is what makes our world. This world may not be the perfect place to live in for some, and yet we must learn to adapt to its transitory moods for our personal growth. This realization brought me to accepting what is unchangeable, and adapting to what is inevitable in my life. Meditation helped me to alter my attitude to the people and situations detrimental to my progress in my life. Well, you might ask, how?

While learning to meditate we are constantly disturbed by the noise outside and our thoughts inside. There seems to be an unending tug-of-war between the outside noise and our endeavor to hold our focus inside. We face this struggle only in the beginning. With time, our mind settles with accepting the noise outside rather than fighting against it anymore. Remember that this is only a temporary acceptance, and not identifying ourselves with them. This attitude acknowledging the existence of the hostile forces outside us while still having an unwavering focus on our goal has helped me in all walks of my life.

Summary

You cannot take charge of your life unless you realize who you are—your mind's infinite potentials and life's countless possibilities. You can discover more about yourself only when you cultivate a habit of voluntarily secluding yourself daily and rise above your incessant thought processes, for a few minutes daily. This state of your mental relaxation, no matter how brief, is like a balcony of your life's mansion wherefrom you can perceive the daily events of your life and your position in every relationship better and more objectively.

Meditation, a discipline of voluntary silence, promising more clarity in your thinking, poise in your conduct and prudence in your decisions, some of the cardinal qualities needed in our nature to better understand our day-to-day life and take its charge.

- - - - - - - - - -

Highlights of
A Way To Take Charge of Your Life

(1)   The more we have endeavored to touch the distant planets, the more we have lost touch with our own. The more we have searched for success out in the world, the more we have lost harmony within ourselves.

(2)   For the lasting success and deepest fulfillment in our lives, all changes in the area of our **self-improvement must occur from within,** and not in our outer behavior alone. Meditation promises this result.

(3)   Altering our mind's focus, from its habitual thought processes, to the state of our inner silence now and then, helps heighten our perception to better perceive our daily events and prioritize more rightly our daily demands.

(4)   A study of spiritual masters and great thinkers will reveal that they possess one thing in common: A realization of the power of mental solitude; a voluntary seclusion—a seat of profound thoughts, guidance, comfort and rare experiences.

(5)   Regardless of the varied names given to it by different faiths, the only purpose of meditation is to calm our ever-turbulent mind and develop a better perception of the circumstances, relationships and events in our lives at a given moment.

(6)   Call it by any name, a heighten sense of perception, wisdom, insight, prudence or intuitive feeling, it cannot be learned in classrooms of conventional schools, universities or seminars. It comes only through our self-realization, which is the aim of meditation.

= = = = = =

2

MEDITATIVE VISUALIZATION

*"You rise as high as the influence
of a person of your inspiration."*
(Paramahansa Yogananda)

I do not promote meditation as a practice to attain a mental state of thoughtlessness, as some believe. This however may be the pursuit of those who have dedicated their lives to a certain way of living, particularly from their early age under the guidance of an experienced teacher.

To me, meditation is training our mind to focus on such an object that infuses in us the desired qualities such as calmness, solace and rejuvenation. It is not rising above our thoughts entirely and focusing on some state of emptiness, which if not impossible, is certainly a very difficult task, especially for those like you and me who have to carry out countless responsibilities in their daily lives. Meditation is disciplining our mind to shifting its focus and hold it longest to our capacity to enjoy the benefits, mainly that of enjoying relaxation.

I have discussed, in the interest of the serious students, different methods of meditation in the following section. The present chapter is in the general interest of those who want to make meditation a part of their daily life, and also those who want to simply try it out without a sense of commitment.

All those like you and me interested in altering themselves from within generally begin with a practice of this nature, and then grow into practicing one of the structured ones shown later in the next section. Meditative visualization needs no teacher, guru or regiment of rules. It does not require having faith in God or sitting in a particular physical posture. It does not require finding a quiet spot or setting a timepiece to remind you of the end of the practice. These things benefit the practice of course, but are needed more by those who are serious with enriching their lives and have developed faith in this discipline.

This brief practice, as its benefits become obvious in your life, may eventually turn into a part of your daily life. A wise person is the one who constantly looks out for the ways in the personal growth, beyond one's age and conditioned lifestyle. Once your practice matures, further guidance and tips for your further progress will come to you from within naturally. The technique discussed here is simple and easy to practice, anywhere anytime.

This practice requires you to withdraw your attention, from the outside world of objects, to your inside world, from others to yourself. Sit in a place where you may face minimal distraction, close your eyes and hold your attention on to a focus projecting positive influences. It is a conscious effort of comfortably sitting in a quite place and directing your mind on to the qualities of the object of your focus, which may help to relax and inspire you. I have discussed more about the objects of focus in the following paragraphs.

Selection of Focus

Selecting a focus is of profound importance in

practicing visualization. From the millions of objects of desires in the outside world, and people and experiences in your personal life, choose the one that may awaken in you some positive influence. Your focus may be someone you most admire, love or adore; someone you look up to for strength and comfort; someone endowed with superior human qualities such as courage, valor and compassion; someone you idolize and very much wish to be like eventually.

You could also focus on nature's panorama such as the sunrise, a waterfall, a full moon night or a rainbow that projects qualities of glory, tranquility and purity to refresh and calm your mind. The focus could also be on a pleasant memory of your past or a vision of your future. In brief, your mind should be carefully withdrawn from the negative sources, and directed to a particular focus, which may be in the form of a person, an object or experience, a nature's scene, memory or a vision for creating in your mind the corresponding feeling such as peace, joy, serenity or a sense of personal upliftment.

We encounter several such incidents in our daily lives that project the principle of this technique. Family pictures on our desks at work, grandparents' portraits in homes, pictures of leaders and nature's scenes hanging on office walls, especially in corporate lounges and training rooms. The sight of these pictures directly influences our minds and blood circulation. It loosens our stress, softens our tension, mellows our moods, and fills our minds with strength, courage, inspiration and peace. The changed mental attitude and moods create corresponding effects in our health.

This technique of meditative visualization is similar to the art of visualization or a guided imagery often used by athletes and recommended in the workshops of losing weight, automatic writing, making money, public speaking and preparing for job interviews. Common to both techniques is an act of mental rehearsal wherein practitioners identify themselves with the qualities of the focal point and mentally imbibe them. This can be practiced anywhere, on a plane or bus, between meetings and appointments. It takes only a few minutes, and yet promises to bring immense benefits.

The Technique Is Simple and Beneficial

This method of meditative visualization differs from other techniques of visualization in three ways: its ultimate purpose, object of focus, and accepting the presence of our higher mind. The ultimate purpose of this method is of self-transformation, beyond the material gains. The purpose is to bring more qualities such as love, joy and peace into our lives. An attainment of such internal change takes much of our patience and persistence.

Certain discipline may become redundant after their purposes are served. A dietary discipline or that of physical exercise, for examples, may grow unnecessary after its purpose is met, say of losing the desired amount of weight. Whereas, a discipline aimed at one's self-transformation grows with time an integral part of one's life even after the purpose is seemingly met. Meditative visualization is one of such techniques, which gradually becomes a life long discipline for attaining and retaining its benefits.

There are three levels of human mind, conscious, subconscious and higher or super-conscious mind. When we use the phrase as "I have trained my mind," or "the great ones discipline their mind from an early age," the question may arise, "Which is the *trained mind* and which is the *training mind*?" Our conscious mind is often undisciplined and chaotic. If we want to put it to work in a right direction and obtain optimal production from it, we cannot leave it to itself. We must invite the power of our higher mind, which has a natural ability to distinguish between right and wrong, and disciplinarian by nature.

Our higher mind is also known as our higher self, higher power or intuitive faculty. Sitting in this practice for a minute or two in a prayerful or contemplative mood, before leading our mind to the desired focus promotes higher level of our endurance of focus, and reaping results, faster than otherwise.

Practice this particular method for about fifteen minutes preferably before leaving your home in the morning. Once you get a handle of it, you can practice it anywhere and anytime. You can practice meditation while sitting in your bed or recliner, at home or while resting in your car during your lunch break. You can do it while commuting on a bus, plane or train, or while waiting for your train or airplane. You can easily slip into your practice for few minutes while others around you are engaged into reading, talking, eating and resting.

This will help you train your mind and reap the benefits faster without making special efforts to spare time from your busy life.

Watch Out the Two Challenges

After you have selected the object to focus on, keep your mind anchored to it. Our mind by its nature resists every discipline until it is harnessed. I wish to caution you here about a couple of challenges that your mind may pose to you in the beginning. One, its rebellious nature may dissuade you from the practice, and two, its tendency to frequently waver from its focus.

Accept the fact that our untrained mind resists every new discipline. Do not feel therefore discouraged when it acts contrary to your frequent attempts. This should only happen for few days in the beginning. Once you persist in your determination your mind will drop its resistance. The relationship between our mind and us is like that of a new animal and trainer in the circus, strife and struggle in the beginning turning later into a trusting friendship.

Another challenge is of holding your mind on to the selected focus. Whenever your mind wavers, gently bring it back to its focus. Do not wrangle or wrestle with it like a boxer treating his opponent in the ring. Treat it more like a mother to her child, gentle by heart but disciplinarian by attitude, reprimanding her child for its misconduct gently but in firm words.

One fringe benefit that I used to enjoy, while working for an organization many years ago, was the availability of a small chapel on the premises. I often used to spend a few minutes of my lunch breaks in that chapel. The quiet and blissful ambiance of the chapel under dim lights proved to be very conducive to taking my mind off the pressures of the workday.

Though mentioned earlier that meditative visualization can be practiced anywhere and anytime time of the day, I would like however to share with you the way that I once used to practice and enjoyed the benefit of holding steady my focus in my early period of discipline. Endured focus is very important, besides choosing a right image for focus, to absorb the qualities of the image at the deepest level possible in our mind. Sit wherever and however you may feel comfortable, on the floor, in a chair or in your car.

A Way to Practice

Focus on your pupils behind your closed eyes. You will notice them restless and fluttering. Observe them for few seconds to enable them to slowly hold still. Remember that our thoughts and movement of our pupils have a direct connection. The state of our pupils expresses the state of our thoughts. It is the same what we call REM, the Rapid Eye Movement, while our mind is in its subconscious state during our sleep.

You may not be aware of that regulating the movement of our pupils helps regulate our thoughts. Let me try to explain it differently. You know that our physical behavior expresses our mental attitude at a given moment. When it is difficult to alter the mental attitude from within, one can bring a desired alteration by altering one's outer behavior.

After your thoughts calm down little, lead your attention to the center between your eyes. This is the seat of our higher mind. Let your mind focus here for a minute or two. The mental focus at this spot, with the highest concentration possible, will act like gentle knocks on the portal of your higher mind to awaken it. This is the centerpiece of this technique. Now create here the desired image for your focus.

This image could be of any object, person or memory as discussed earlier. Hold this focus as long as you can. Very likely, you will soon waver from the focus. That's fine. Accept it as natural. As soon as you become aware of your deviation from the focus, lead your attention back to the image. Keep persisting. This is the only way to train what we call the mind, and awaken our higher mind without whose help our mind's potentials cannot be fully realized. With time, this battle will naturally reduce.

While holding the focus on your image visualize that your mind is absorbing the qualities of the image. The greater the duration of your focus, the more profound will be the influence on you of the object. Focus on the qualities that your image stands for. Remember that what we perpetually think so we eventually become. **Paramahansa Yogananda** said that our mind is like a crystal, which has a natural tendency to pick up the shape and color of the object nearest it. Psychologists may contend that a human mind is made of the infinite layers of impressions gathered during its lifetime.

In one of my seminars, a participant once asked me whether she could make the image of Virgin Mary as her focus in meditative visualization. "Absolutely," I had promptly responded. I truly encourage others having the images of divine entities, if they have that kind of faith. Where shall we ever find the images so pure and perfect in all respects like the ones of the gods and goddesses? Know that the result of the visualization depends on the image you select for your focus. Having the image of someone who is immensely embodied with the qualities that we deeply admire speeds our progress effortlessly.

Summary

This technique of meditative visualization is based on a simple principle of psychology that our mind possesses a natural tendency to absorb the qualities of the object it associates with, like a piece of crystal reflects the color and shape of the object nearest it. If you find it difficult to calm your thoughts, it must not despair or frustrate you. The primary focus in the practice is identifying yourself with the qualities of the object of your focus.

- - - - - - - - - -

Highlights of
Meditative Visualization

(1) Holding the image at the center between your closed eyes, with the deepest concentration possible, act like knocking, subtly but firmly, on the portal of your higher mind to awaken it. This is the secret of this technique.

(2) Not until you recognize the supremacy of your higher mind, the seat of your will power, over your conscious mind, will you be able to enjoy the full benefits of this or any other discipline, bringing the desired success in your life.

(3) Remember that what we perpetually think of so we eventually become. Psychologists contend that a human mind is made of the infinite layers of impressions gathered during its lifetime. Try to focus therefore only on the positive and inspiring factors in life, yours and other's.

= = = = = = = = = =

THE SEVEN IMPORTANT TIPS

"Learn to be silent,
Let your quiet mind listen and absorb."
(Pythagoras, A Greek Philosopher)

This chapter discusses seven important tips to hold your focus longer and enjoy the benefits of the practice to its fullest. This chapter will also help you to better understand the different methods of meditation and their benefits, discussed at length in the next four chapters. These methods, however, require more sincerity and level of concentration compared to the technique of meditative visualization that you learned in the previous chapter. The difference between the two is this: meditative visualization does not require one to be seriously attentive to some of the preliminaries such as one's physical posture, way of breathing and choosing the venue while practicing to the extent as suggested in other methods discussed in the next section of this book.

Integrating these tips into your regular practice, at least during your initial period, will make your meditation a more pleasant experience, lasting longer than otherwise, relieving your frustration that beginners often experience. The more diligently you incorporate these tips into your daily practice, the more effortlessly you may find your mind immersing into the state of relaxation. To those like me whose lifestyle is

generally sedentary, this regiment of simple exercises
will bring an added benefit of improved health through
activating their body cells and physiological processes.

The initial period in every discipline is critical. For
this reason, I have dedicated this chapter fully to those
tips, which have helped me anchor into practicing
meditation for years, and I follow them as diligently as
possible even today. I hope that they may help you as
well to form a foundation for your practice.
Furthermore, observing these tips will encourage you
to assign a particular hour of the day and place for your
daily meditation, and foster a greater sense of
appreciation of the benefits of meditation.

The Five Tips Before Meditation

(1) *A Warm-Up Exercise*, in the beginning of your
   practice, will prove highly beneficial.

This exercise contains two parts: stretching and
breathing. The very title is self-explanatory; stretching,
straining and letting go the parts of your body. I have
endeavored to describe the way I used to follow these
exercises in my early days of the practice. Read the entire
chapter first before getting into the practice of
meditation, especially if you are a beginner. My normal
recommendation is to repeat each exercise for about five
times. Nevertheless, you may modify the exercises in
ways and repetitions depending on your comfort level.
You know your health better than others.

(a) Stretching :

✦ To start, stand straight with your hands on your
   waist. Pull your shoulders backward, stretch your
   chest forward and have your abdomen squeezed
   inward. During this position, tense as many parts

of your body, from head to toes, you can in turn, hold each tensed position as long as you can comfortably, and then let it go. Repeat this—tensing, holding and letting go—for about five times.

✦ After completing the first exercise, try to raise your body on your toes, and hold this position as long and comfortably as you can. You may need the support of a chair or wall for your balance. When you cannot hold this position any longer, return to normal position, and repeat. Repeat this for five times.

✦ You should now be able to bend forward as far as you can to touch your toes with your hands. If your hands cannot reach all the way to your toes, do not worry. Take your hands down as far as you can in the direction of your toes. Remain in this position for few seconds and return to your normal standing position. Repeat for about five times.

✦ Stretch your hands straight in front of you, with your palms facing each other forming a ninety-degree angle to your body. Try to keep your arms as stretched as possible. Hold this position for thirty seconds or so. Now turn your hands outward, opposite to each other, and slowly sweep your arms from your shoulders behind your back until they are fully outstretched to your comfort level. Stay in this position for thirty seconds or so. This completes one cycle—stretching your arms forward and holding, stretching them backward and holding again. Repeat this cycle five times. Do not overexert or overstretch. Pay attention to your comfort level.

✦ Now, sit on the floor or in a chair where you will later continue your meditation. Slowly roll your head clockwise for five times, and then anti-clockwise again for five times. Rhythm and gentleness, in place of accidental jerks and rush, are necessary in this exercise. This will tone and massage the area of your throat and neck.

The back of your neck is very important part of our body. Physiologically, it forms the meeting point of our spine and medulla oblongata, and is quite vulnerable when the stress in our lives grows unmanageable. I may add to your knowledge that according to the science of the *Kundalini Yoga*, our throat is a seat of the fifth, of the seven *charkas*, the psychic energy centers in our bodies, known as the *vishuddha* or throat charka. I have discussed this topic to your interest elsewhere in this book.

This warm-up exercise will strain all your body from its head through toes—the arms, shoulders, rib cage, legs, back, joints and nerves—further activating its physiological processes such as of breathing, drawing more oxygen, blood circulation and producing more chemicals in your body. The more supple and tension-free is your body, the more the ability it gains to sit longer and steadily in your desired position and holding mental concentration. This brief exercise possesses potential to enable your experience the state of relaxation at a deeper level than otherwise.

(b) The Breathing exercise is as simple as the stretching one. Follow it with your common sense. You alone are the best judge of your body, health and temperament.

Sit, still and upright to your comfort level. Inhale slowly and deeply to fill up your lungs through your nose and exhale with a force through your mouth. Again, inhale slowly and deeply through your nose and exhale with force through your mouth. Follow this process about ten times, and then resume to your natural way of breathing. This will enable your lungs to draw more air, strengthen their muscles and expand them evermore. When doing this exercise in a cleaner environment the deeper breathing brings in more oxygen into our system, gradually changing our breathing pattern to more diaphragmatic and rhythmic. A high level of oxygenated blood promotes health to our cells both of physiology and brain. This exercise of breathing benefits our overall health, helping us hold our focus longer in meditation.

I recommend to do both the stretching and breathing parts of the warm-up exercise, if at all possible. Combined, they may take only about seven minutes. Nevertheless, under the pressure of time, if a choice has to be made between the two, I suggest you to go for the breathing exercise. This exercise will largely contribute to making your meditation a pleasant experience, and the latter will set the tone of your day.

(2) Choose Your Venue Carefully for your privacy and quietude. A quiet environment is more conducive to your practice. It will help your mind rise above its material consciousness and tune in with your mental focus with greater ease. Often, in an early stage of every discipline, external environment is more influential than our personal resolves. Therefore, choose such a spot that may be clean and free of distraction as much possible to further boost up your mood to meditate.

(3) Set Your Alarm to go off about fifteen minutes after you start your practice or seek someone's help to remind you. This will free your mind from the anxiety of losing track of your time. After your mental clock is accordingly programmed with time, you may not need the timepiece any more. A better suggestion, however, is to find a quieter substitute to an alarm clock. In my early period of practice, I used to keep my tiny timepiece a few feet away from my seat, or wrapped in a towel

or small blanket to keep its sound just barely audible, and it would stop by itself after sending out a signal twice.

If you practice regularly, and preferably, at the same hour of the day or night, your mental clock will take over the function of your physical timepiece after a few days. I have seen people who can wake up in the morning, independent to external aids, precisely at the time they had promised to themselves before going to bed the previous night. I have also succeeded in training my mind in this discipline. You can learn it too with time and practice.

I might add that just as there is a human made clock, which regulates our day-to-day life, I have encountered the mentions of the biological clock, a mental clock and a cosmic clock. Our physiological cells and organs function with certain rhythm and frequencies. In a healthy adult body, the heart pumps about 70 times, the pair of lungs expands and contracts 18 times per minute, and the average life span of a red cell in our blood is said to be 120 days. Such physiological functions in our bodies are regulated by the so-called biological clock.

Those who are highly evolved spiritually or have developed advanced psychic abilities possess the knowledge of how the cosmic clock operates. This is how they can predict major events in human life and also, the precise days and hours of their occurrences. The astrological science is based on this clock. As one's inner silence deepens in one's meditative practice, one begins realizing the knowledge of these things naturally. Those who have attained psychic powers are well aware of one thing—**the power of inner silence, the only way to effectively connect to the higher power in their lives.**

(4) *A Right Posture* facilitates our body to remain
steady in a certain position, and our mind to stay
focused longer. It is our experience that adjusting our
physical posture, comfortable but suitable to the
purpose at a given moment, helps us accomplish our
undertaking more effectively. While working from 9 to
5 we are sitting in one posture, while entertaining
ourselves in the front of a television show we are sitting
in a different posture, and while praying we are sitting
in a posture different altogether. We modify our
postures, depending upon what we are engaged into
at a given moment, helping us perform better and with
the utmost ease.

In a like manner, when meditating, our seated
position should be as comfortable and conducive to the
purpose of our discipline. Sit straight up on the floor,
or lean against the wall to support your back. Sit in a
chair, recliner or couch, if that suits you more. Do not
be over concerned about your posture during the
beginning of your practice. What is more important is
how comfortably and steadily you can sit. My physical
posture, since the day I began practicing some 20 years
ago, is still the same. I sit on the floor with my legs
folded and arms resting on my knees. Everybody's needs
and level of adaptability are different.

Paramahansa Yogananda writes that struggling to
maintain a certain physical posture is not essential for
meditation, but it can certainly accelerate one's
progress. A bent posture is dangerous to the spine
because it may throw its discs or vertebrae off their
alignment. Moreover, a bent posture may pinch a nerve
retarding the flow of energy, like a water-hose, squeezed
in the middle, obstructs the flow of water.

I suggest you to pay attention to two things. First,
do not attempt to meditate while lying in bed because
such a position has a tendency to induce a stupor,

making your practice counter effective of its purpose. You may do so however under a proper supervision. Lying flat on the back to meditate, with a focus on one's breathing, is called the *Savãsanã*, the corpse-posture, in Buddhism. A teacher instructs his students to practice this method of meditation only when they have successfully demonstrated a prolonged state of inner awareness.

Second, make sure that your feet rest on the floor or footrest when in the practice. You may sit on the floor or in a chair with your spine comfortably firm against its back. This is one of the ten important tips, which most books and workshops on this subject overlook to mention. (You will find the list of the ten tips in the back of this book for your quick reference and reminder.) Once you are settled in your practice, your body will exercise its own intelligence in forming a position suitable to your longer state of relaxation. Remember that meditation is a psychological discipline, more than a physical one.

(5) Maintaining a Positive Attitude is a necessary factor for the desired success in all areas of our lives. I do not think anyone needs to tell you more about this. Picking up this book is a testimony that you already possess a high level of positive attitude. You would not be serious otherwise about finding more ways to improve your life, especially when the general attitude of most people is to change others rather than changing themselves. However, we all need to be reminded now and then of who we are, how we are progressing, and how to be what we can be.

Keeping a sustained positive attitude, especially in the area of self-transformation is often difficult. Therefore, be very careful to orient your mind with a good attitude every time you start your meditation. Do not doubt the effects of meditation. Remind yourself whenever you begin your practice with something like this: "Meditation has helped millions in their lives, and so it will help me too." I write this out of my personal experience.

Our positive attitude is everything. It is an essential component to make the best of every discipline, whether with worldly success or a personal journey. Unfounded doubts and fears are highly detrimental to our progress. Focus more instead, on the very inspiring thought that drew you on to this path.

The Two Tips After Meditation

(6) *Relive The Crescendo Effect* of peace that you enjoyed in your meditation. After the timepiece goes off, stay seated for a little while peacefully, maybe a minute or two. During this brief period, focus on to the peak experience during your meditation you had enjoyed. This experience lasts, in the beginners, only for a little while; it could be just for few seconds or only for a fraction of a moment. The duration of the experience is insignificant. The whole purpose is to bring back that experience to your conscious level and relive it.

Reliving the memory of this experience for a couple of minutes, or longer depending on your level of interest developed in the practice will enable your mind to further absorb its influence. It is recapturing the pleasant moment of peace, joy, exaltation or whatever experienced, and reinforce its impression in your mind. This will facilitate you to summon the said experience to your rescue when you feel caught in a stressful situation during your busy day. This exercise may prove immensely effective in your meditation as well as in other aspects of your life.

It could also happen that you may not have any such experience at all. This is not uncommon when you are new to this discipline, or your brain cells are fatigued, or your mind is restless for some reason. Do not be over concerned about it. Just accept the situation. It just happens at times. Remind yourself however that the aim of your meditation is not chasing an experience of a certain nature. In my experience, the more we chase it, the more we miss it. Let it happen naturally.

You have control over your faith, interest and efforts in your practice, but not on its outcome. If you experience something profound in your meditation, continue sitting in your position a little longer and rejoice in the memory of the experience. It will be of immense benefit to you. If you did not have any such experience at all to recall, I advise that you still remain seated nonjudgmental. Never feel frustrated for not having the immediate desired effect of meditation or lose motivation to practice again next day. If your mind has developed faith and persistence, it will surely attain the desired state.

(7) *Thank Your Higher Power* as a concluding gesture of your practice. It is my conviction that there prevails in the universe a power, in the form of some universal intelligent energy, which influences our lives according to our attitudes and level of faith in it. It governs our universe and maintains a balance of the good and evil in it. It keeps a precise account of all our deeds, good and bad alike, and declares judgments accordingly through its laws, as for example, the law of karma.

Ralph Waldo Emerson expressed the same tone differently in his *Compensation*:

"The world looks like a mathematical equation, which turn anyhow you will, balances itself. Every secret is told, every crime is punished, every virtue is rewarded, and every wrong is redressed, in silence and certainty."

This is the cosmic energy as I refer to, without whose grace the rare experiences that we enjoy in our meditative silence is simply impossible. We may attach different names to this universal intelligence according to our faiths and personal experiences. When doing wrong, some voice from within us warns us, when taking a wrong "exit" in our life's journey some invisible hand from within takes over our life's steering and guides us. When passing through a dark tunnel in some period of our life, someone invisibly holds a torch for us. If you have ever encountered such an experience even once in your life, know it as the manifestation of the same universal intelligence or cosmic energy I am referring to. You may call it your higher power.

Summary

These are only suggestions drawn mainly from my own experiences. They will help you to speed your progress in meditation, and also prevent the level of despair and frustration that some new practitioners, without a proper guidance and supervision, often experience. While practicing the instructions suggested in this chapter be mindful of your body's responses at every stage. Do not observe them literarily because everyone's body responds differently. With this consideration in your mind, if you integrate this set of exercises into your regular practice, I assure you that it will double your progress in meditation.

- - - - - - - - -

Highlights of
The Seven Important Tips

(1) Integrating these tips into your regular practice, at least for a few weeks in the beginning, will help head start your meditation with a pleasant experiences.

(2) The stretching and breathing exercises combined will set the tone of your meditation, making your mind relaxed, and reliving the crescendo effect of meditation will set the tone of your day, keeping you poise more than otherwise.

(3) The warm-up exercise will help you, not only to sit and endure your focus more steadily, it will also improve your health.

(4) Based on my experience, the more you are tuned in to thanking your higher power at the end of your meditation, irrespective of the level of experience you had in your practice, the more you will be able to attract the experiences positively and effortlessly in your life. It will set the tone of your rest of day.

= = = = = =

SECTION II

The Four Methods, and The Living Meditation

Chapter 4
MEDITATION ON BREATHING

Chapter 5
MEDITATION ON MUSIC

Chapter 6
MEDITATION ON THOUGHTS

Chapter 7
MEDITATION ON "MANTRA"

Chapter 8
THE LIVING MEDITATION

SECTION II

THE FOUR METHODS OF MEDITATION

Introduction

We discussed in the previous section the concepts of meditation, meditative visualization and the seven tips of meditation. In this section, I have presented four methods of meditation, each aiming at bringing you the same benefit in its final pursuit, taking your mind away from your day-to-day demands for a little while so as you may develop an altered perception of your daily events. At the same time, each method differs from the other methods in its focus during the practice. Choose one that may best suit your health, temperament, mental proclivities and lifestyle.

The Four Methods:

(1) Meditation on **Breathing**,
(2) Meditation on **Music**,
(3) Meditation on **Thoughts**, and
(4) Meditation on *Mantra*.

In this section, I have dedicated to each method one full chapter. Each chapter discusses about the concept and significance of the focus, steps to practice, and other details pertinent to drawing the most out of practicing the particular method. Each chapter also includes my personal experiences in this journey. You may find some of the steps and tips of meditation being repeated. I have allowed this to occur with a purpose, to helping you, as a reader, enjoy the flow in reading, instead of flipping the pages back and forth for reference now and again. Moreover, it reinforces the values of those steps and tips.

MEDITATION ON BREATHING

"To go very far, you must begin very near
and near is you, the 'you' that you must understand."
(J. Krishnamurti)

Breathing Is More Than A Living

Abreath is a bridge, nature's umbilical cord, tied at one end to our physical body and at the other end to what we call life. Breath sustains and nurtures every life from its birth through its death. When breath leaves, life leaves. The very moment a child's umbilical cord is severed, Mother Nature takes over the role of the child's biological mother to supply air, the life-force to the newborn.

The instant the newborn is left to be independent from its mother; its first cry is for hanging on to the supply of life, and not for food or love. The child realizes the importance of these needs later in its life. In the books on the science of yoga, breath is called the *prana*, the vital life force, and the process of taking in and taking out of breath is called the *pranayama*, meaning a regulation of the life force.

The pattern of our breathing determines the quality of our health and longevity. Let me offer you some real life instances. An adult human averagely breathes 18 times per minute, and lives to be around 70 years old.

A monkey, known as restless by its nature, breathes averagely 32 times per minute and lives 20 years. And finally, a turtle, that averagely breathes about 4 times a minute only, and outlives the human beings and monkeys in longevity to over 150 years. You may arrive at two points out of these illustrations. **One, the less frequently is the breathing, the longer is the life span, and two, the deeper is the breathing, the greater is the temperamental composure.**

The science of yoga had long discovered, and modern medical science now validates, that our way of breathing directly influences our health, temperament and longevity. Those who breathe deeply and rhythmically enjoy overall better health, mental composure and longevity compared to their counterparts. A pattern of diaphragmatic breathing supplies more oxygen to our body rendering it a longer and healthier life. This way of natural breathing produces endorphins, a natural pain killer substance in our brains, which boosts our natural immunity against our sensation of pains.

Breathing, in a sense, is a reminder to us of our life and death. Inhalation represents life and exhalation, death. The first inhalation of a child means a life to it, the last exhalation of a person means the end of his or her life. This repetitive cycle of inhaling and exhaling is the process of life in, and life out, in a human body. Focusing on this process of breath flowing in and flowing out of our bodies while meditating, reminds us of some power greater than our own body and mind. This state of realization maybe even just for a little while but possesses potential to last longer as our practice matures with time.

Awareness of breath as the focal point of our practice is called the *Vipasana* in Buddhism, meaning *seeing the events as they are*. This focus helps us to gradually rise above our attachment to our body, and as a result, the petty physical aches, pains and discomforts grow less disturbing to us. This process of gradual dissociation from our body-consciousness, and increasing association with our breathing, the basic source of life, enables us to grow more immune to the influences of the sources of anxiety, anger and hypertension in our daily life.

The focus on our breath also enhances our psychophysical immunity. Do you know what technique was used some hundred years ago to make the patients suffer less pain while passing through a surgical procedure? Before the invention of chloroform and anesthesia, patients were first instructed on a breathing exercise prior to undergoing a surgery. These instructions in breathing were meant to encourage patients to shift their attention from their bodies, which would help desensitize their minds from their pains during the surgery. The patients would hold their focus on their breaths, as long as possible while being operated on.

The pregnant mothers when delivering their babies, whether in modern cities or primitive societies, are encouraged by the attending professionals to focus on their breathing. They are asked to breathe as deeply as possible to help them deliver the child naturally, and assuage the pains associated to it. You can see, in our daily lives, the benefits of breathing when disciplined. They prove one thing clearly that when our mind is trained to focus on our life-force, our breaths; it naturally grows unmindful of the pains and discomforts in our physical bodies.

Breathing, Psychic Powers and Dangers

I wish to share with you, in some length, how our breathing when disciplined and practiced with a proper guidance, helps speed up our spiritual progress and activate the *chakras,* energy centers in our body, for attaining material success in our lives. These *chakras* when activated unlock our potentials, making us realize the worldly riches and fame in our lives. Such powers of a disciplined breathing are elaborately discussed in the books on the *Kundalini Yoga,* one of the ancient schools in the science of yoga. This school of yoga announces the seven metaphorical energy centers located along the passage of our spines, known as the *chakras* in the Sanskrit language, meaning the wheels, vortexes or energy centers.

In this chapter, we shall refer to these *chakras* as the energy centers. These energy centers are normally inactive, or sluggish in motion, in an average human being. When these wheels are activated they begin spinning, normally starting with the lowest one located at the base of the spine, called the *muladhar chakra,* the base energy center.

With the activation of the energy centers, the practitioners begin experiencing the psychic powers associated with the respective centers, demonstrating such qualities that they might have rarely thought of. Premonition, precognition, clairvoyance, reading others' thoughts or projecting own, and demonstrating a high level of concentration, or recollection of memory are some of the examples of these psychic abilities. An undue attention to these psychic powers may simply distract the students who are still learning to relax in their practice.

Activating even one energy center is capable of bringing about amazing progress in the practitioners' lives, which otherwise, would not be possible at all, or take several years of hard work to attain it. The lower three centers are connected to the worldly fame, wealth and material success. **Gopi Krishna** writes,

"...Kundalini, is the real cause of all genuine spiritual and psychic phenomena, the biological basis of evolution and development of personality...." The middle one, *anahat chakra*, located in the heart region, is the seat of our mental tranquility, poise and balance in life. The upper three, located respectively in the throat, forehead, and the crown region are known for our psychic powers and spiritual progress.

Let us see how our breathing helps activate these centers and develop our potentials. Normally, the student begins with inhaling deeply and exhaling forcefully through his mouth, while holding his mental focus on the object advised by his teacher. As you may know there are four stages in a complete breathing cycle: Inhalation, inner retention, exhalation, and outer retention. Just before exhaling and inhaling again, you may notice a brief pause, almost imperceptible. This is natural retention of breath. Each of the four stages equally contributes to activating the *chakras*, and the teacher asks his student, depending on his overall health and interest, to concentrate on a particular stage of breathing. No two students, even of the same age, sometimes get identical instructions.

This technique of activating the centers should be learned from an experienced teacher who can better understand the intricacies and dangers of this particular discipline of the yoga. A teacher guides his students depending on their ages, nature of health, and the levels of concentration and spiritual orientation developed. I caution you against practicing this or any such discipline in which the primary focus is on developing your energy centers. I emphasize this because there are many dangers, including mental disorders, if there is no proper coordination of good health, right focus in the practice and proper instruction from the teacher. This happened to **Gopi Krishna,** a young aspirant caught into developing his psychic powers.

While practicing the instructions learned from the lay books on yoga, Gopi Krishna led himself to such a stage in his practice where he began experiencing insanity of his mind and several disorders in his health. As a young boy, in a quest to prove himself to be something to his family and peers, he was mesmerized by the quick ways of awakening the psychic centers in his body. When he was about 17 years old, he began meditating every morning, for a couple of hours in a single session, practicing the instructions that he had learned from the books. After some 17 years of his practice, he began experiencing such adverse effects in his both body and mind that he found himself totally at loss of their cures.

It seemed that the untimely released force of energy had thrown off the balance of the electric system in his body. In *KUNDALINI, The Evolutionary Energy in Man*, **Gopi Krishna** writes, "I felt exhausted and spent...I suffered loss of appetite, and food tasted like ash in my mouth.... I lost my regularity and found myself at the mercy of a new released force about which I knew nothing...." (Pg 51)

Gopi Krishna further describes his condition in the following words :

" [when] the awakening [of the Kundalini, the psychic energy] occurs suddenly at some period in life, more often than not end in mental disorder, which makes a coherent narration of the experience impossible. Under the circumstances it is no wonder that a detailed account of this strange experience in not available anywhere." (Pg 114)

Developing the psychic powers should never be a primary purpose of your meditative practice. They will come on their own accord, as a result of the progress in your meditation. It is like happiness, which ensues naturally once we are on the right path and possess a right perception of life. Those who make it their primary goal simply miss it like chasing a rainbow in vain.

The serious students of meditation may also find another favorite book of mine on this subject: *The SERPENT POWER* by **Arthur Avalon** (Sir John Woodruff). This brief discussion about the *chakras* is mainly to remind you of the influence of our breathing on our worldly success and accomplishments. It is also to show you the dangers in doing on your own without proper directions from an experienced teacher.

Once you anchor yourself daily into some regular discipline aimed at enjoying a few minutes of peace, further guidance will begin coming to you effortlessly. I have personally experienced this on several occasions. **The Bible** makes a similar reference: Seek and you will find, ask and you will receive, knock and it will open. The sole purpose of your meditation in the beginning should be of attaining mental relaxation.

Steps to Practice

If you are reading this chapter after many days from the time you last read the chapter three, I suggest you that you review the latter for the seven important tips to make your practice a more beneficial.

(a) Do the warm-up exercise: stretching and breathing.

(b) Choose your surroundings carefully. Prefer a quieter environment.

(c) Sit comfortably to help you maintain your correct posture for a longer, steadier focus.

(d) Set your timer to remind you to end your practice after about fifteen minutes.

(e) Begin your practice with a positive attitude. Raise your mind, for the duration of your practice at least, above its usual state of doubting and worrying.

(f) Close your eyes. Lead your attention gently at the point between your eyebrows and focus on your breaths. Now, slowly begin to count your exhalation one through fifteen. Watch your breath going in, and when it goes out count one. Thus continue your normal breathing process and adding one to your count every time you breathe out. When I was new to meditation, this exercise used to take me a couple of minutes, longer than now, because of my mind's tendency to frequently waver. When your mind wavers do not be discouraged.

(g) Now, gradually shift your awareness to your breathing. Watch the complete cycle of your breathing: the breath is flowing in through your nostrils, reaching your lungs, your abdomen is inflating, natural stillness of your breath for a few seconds, your abdomen is now slowly deflating, your breath is flowing out, and again the natural stillness of your breath for a few seconds before another inhalation. This makes a full cycle of your breathing. Be mindful of every stage of this cycle. Simply watch each stage of the airflow.

Be non-judgmental; only be alert at every stage while watching your breathing. This is all what is expected of you for about ten minutes.

After your alarm goes off:

(h) Release your focus from the center of your eyes and let it settle naturally. Relive, for a moment or so,

again with your eyes closed, the peak experience
your mind had enjoyed; the moment when your
mind was most relaxed. It might have lasted only
for a moment or barely few seconds.

(i) Open your eyes now and be aware of your
surroundings. Be grateful to your higher power,
whether or not you had a desired experience in your
meditation. I bow my head down with reverence,
at this time, before a framed picture of a saint in
my meditation room.

Your practice ends here. Enter the world of your
daily duties and meet them with the best positive
attitude possible.

Summary

A full cycle of breathing comprises of four stages:
Inhalation, inner retention, exhalation and outer
retention. Focus on your breath and be aware of
it at its every stage. The chaotic nature of
breathing, common to all practitioners in the
beginning, will gradually turn into a rhythmic
one, influencing your mental attitude and health
positively. You simply watch each stage of the
airflow objectively and with alertness. Whenever
your mind moves from its focus gently lead it
back to its position, your breath. Carefully refrain
your mind from passing judgments or debating
with itself. Do not expect immediate benefits out
of this, or any other, method of meditation. Every
discipline of self-transformation is a slow process.

- - - - - - - -

Highlights of
Meditation On Breathing

(1) Simply be aware of your breaths with your eyes
     closed and bodily movements infrequently. This
     will lead your mind, gradually and effortlessly, to
     the state of retention, a state between the breaths—
     a higher level of experience.

(2) Focus on the breathing is only a reminder to us of
     the eternal life-and-death process unceasingly
     operating in our lives. Once you realize this you
     naturally grow immune to the unpleasant
     encounters in your life, hostile and detrimental to
     your progress.

(3) Do not focus on the *chakras*, the energy centers,
     while following this method of meditation. Though
     some believe that this method is easier and more
     effective to develop our psychic powers, it may
     cause more harm than good, if practiced
     unsupervised. I cannot emphasize more against its
     practice.

(4) The longer you can hold your focus on your
     breathing, the deeper you will experience the state
     of mental relaxation at the end of your practice.

(5) This method will eventually alter your breathing
     to a more diaphragmatic one, supplying more
     oxygen to your body promoting it more health,
     producing more endorphins to boost your natural
     immunity, and enhancing more composure to your
     mind.

= = = = = =

MEDITATION ON MUSIC

"The right music for you is the one that
stirs you within, beyond your senses. "
(Arun "Yogi" Parekh)

The Origin of Music

L ong ago, our ancestors discovered the influence of
sounds, which successively transformed into what
we call today music. When working in the fields, leading
their livestock and returning home with their herds,
they found their mental moods changing with the
sounds in nature. Each time they heard sounds of winds
blowing, birds flapping wings, clouds thundering,
lightening striking and of raindrops pelting down on
thatched roofs, they experienced an emotional stir deep
within them. They sometimes felt a sense of fright and
at other times a spell of relaxation; sometimes a sense
of exaltation and at other times a sense of despondency.
Some sounds made them happy and exalted, and some
sad and dispirited.

As time passed, the intelligent mind invented
musical instruments to replicate these sounds and
added sound effects to make the sounds more influential
on human emotions, moods and attitudes. Studies show
that under the influence of music, therapeutic treatment
works more effectively, pain is felt less and mothers
suffer less while delivering babies. Research also show

that music calms hypertension, assuage anger, mellow grief and calm violent thoughts. Men march off to war with a song on their lips.

Music has as much power to stir emotions as it does to calm them. It inflames or tramples our sensual appetite. The Bible and Roman literature discuss music as an effective therapeutic device. Music can increase the rate of metabolism in our bodies, change our muscular responses, and produces marked changes in our pulse and blood pressure. The appropriate type of music helps reduce stress and deepen the state of mental relaxation in our lives.

As music influences our health, thoughts and emotions, it similarly enhances our spiritual growth. The sounds of cymbals and gong bells in the Hindu temples and Buddhist pagodas serve this very purpose— to calm or transform thoughts and awaken spiritual experiences in the devotees. Music is considered as a gateway to God. In the East, music accompanies every rite and ritual in social and religious celebrations. Music is appropriately selected for every sacrament from the birth of a child through the funeral rites.

Music touches souls as much as our bodies and minds, and accelerates our spiritual progress. The East has a long and rich tradition of music. If asked what music does to me, I may say: It helps me to get away mentally from the continual demands of my life and leads me to the gateway of the mental world of peace, joy and lights.

Music Influence Plants, Pets and Animals

Music possesses a power to influence in all levels of life, the animals, birds, aquatic creatures, and plants. Plants grow healthier in the environment of certain music and even possess an ability to distinguish classical music from popular pop music. The results of an experiment of music upon plants as demonstrated at Oxford University validate this point.

An experiment conducted on flowers in a laboratory at Oxford University discovered amazing results. In two groups of flowerpots, the same nature of flower seeds were sown, and the same amount of water, temperature, fertilizer and nurturing under the supervision of one caretaker were given to them. Each group was kept in a separate room to observe the influence of a different nature of music played for a certain length of time every day. At the end of five weeks, the findings were recorded as follows: plants growing under the influence of the classical music had produced flowers ampler, healthier and brighter in colors compared to their counterparts growing under the influence of pop music in a separate room.

Experiments also have shown that whales and dolphins, and animals such as horses, elephants, lions and chimpanzees in a circus are found more receptive to being trained under the influence of certain types of music. Studies also show that domestic pets such as dogs, cats and birds are found more playful under the influence of certain type of music.

When less conscious lives such as those of animals and plants can relate to music, there is no surprise about its profound influence in the highly evolved lives of human beings. It deeply impacts all levels of our thinking, feeling, creativity and healing. It helps us to change our thoughts and emotions, and the level of our concentration. Music has been inseparably woven into the tapestry of human life from its conceptual stage through the final stage of its death. Often, we are not aware about it, and those who are, have discovered the ways to manage their moods, temperaments and stress in their lives better than others.

Every human life has a distinct rhythm of its own. One's way of breathing, thinking, feeling and level of health combined forms around one's body a field of vibrations, subtle and unique in its level of frequency, called an electro-magnetic field. This field, also called an aura or a hallow, has its highest concentration around our heads. An aura with its subtle vibrations forms a rhythm which distinguishing its owner from all others. The presence of vibrating waves of the aura is also a reason why every human carries a natural liking for music.

I also see another reason for us having a natural affinity to music. Our first exposure, during our prenatal state, is that of being surrounded by the fluid in our mother's womb. We grow and develop amidst the sounds of the gentle waves of this fluid. As we grow, we relate to music through the influence of this sound of waves. I believe that is why we love music regardless of our age, faith, culture and educational background; the preference of music of course differs.

How To Select The Right Music

Select music that is not necessarily the kind you like, but the kind that encourages you to focus. You may have a strong liking, say for pop or jazz but that may not help your meditation. It may prove to be counter-effective. An environment must be conducive to the purpose of the discipline. All music is good, but each has its own place and purpose. Some types of music are simply a stimulant to our senses and provocative to our desires, some lowers our blood pressure and some heightens it. Some inspire us while marching on to a war and some induce sleep. Pop music evokes a certain effect, jazz another, and classical yet another.

I personally enjoy classical and healing music. The music played while meditating must have a strong influence to penetrate your outer consciousness and touch your deepest core. The music that helps to calm your tumultuous mind, and leads it to an experience of the deepest state of relaxation possible is the right one for you. Irrespective of the types and the number of instruments played, the final blend of its scales and pitches should be such that it invokes in you an altered state of consciousness deeper and more effortlessly everyday.

Judge the effectiveness of music, not by your intellect, but rather by its influence on you. When you are in a store listen to a few discs or cassettes of music first, if possible before you buy. An ideal music for your meditation is the one that harmonizes with your **PMES frequency**, as I occasionally refer to. The PMES is the infusion of our Physical, Mental, Emotional and Spiritual frequencies, which varies from person to person, and also, in the same individual from time to time. This means that music that you enjoy today may not influence you at the same level a year later.

It could also happen that your growing state of relaxation in meditation may make you then independent of the need of music. Listen to the same music for a few days or weeks before you declare it ineffective for your meditation. Sometimes, it takes time to build synchronicity, a rapport between the two, music and its listening mind. An added benefit of this method, over other methods, is that you can carry with you music wherever you go and listen to it whenever you choose for the reinforcement of its effect.

Select music, or its portion, that plays long enough to the desired duration of the practice. If the music is

of the desired length of time, it may replace the need
for an alarm to signal you to end the practice. The music
that I used to play was some twenty-minutes long,
approximately the length of time I had allocated for
meditation. From then on, the alarm has lost its
dominance in my practice.

Steps to Practice

It may help you to once again review the chapter
three, "The Seven Important Tips." It will reinforce the
knowledge of the tips to help you better understand
the steps, and absorb easily into your practice.

(a) Do the warm-up exercise: stretching and breathing.

(b) Choose your surroundings carefully. Prefer a quieter
environment.

(c) Sit comfortably to help you maintain your correct
posture for a longer, steadier focus.

(d) Set your alarm clock to remind you to end your
practice after about fifteen minutes.

(e) Turn the music on.

(f) Begin your practice with a positive attitude. Raise
your mind, at least for the duration of your practice,
above its usual state of doubting and worrying.

(g) Close your eyes. Lead your attention gently at the
point between your eyebrows and focus   on your
breaths. Now, slowly begin to count your exhalation
one through fifteen. Watch your breath going in,
and when it goes out count one. Thus continue your
normal breathing process and adding one to your
count every time your breathe out. When your mind

wavers do not be discouraged. Lead it back gently to its focus.

(h) Now, lead your focus from breaths to music being played. Slowly absorb the music into your mind. As your mind and heart engross into the waves of the music, you will grow oblivious to the distracting noise outside and disturbing thoughts within you. Whenever your mind deviates from its focus, do not fight it. Gently lead it back to music. Your growing awareness of the music will help you outgrow the influences of the detrimental factors to your concentration. The influence of music will gradually penetrate through your outer layers of consciousness both physical and mental, and touch your inner most core. You simply sit with minimal bodily movements, and let the music do its job.

After your alarm goes off:

(h) Relive, for a moment or two, again with your eyes closed, the peak experience your mind had enjoyed; the moment when your mind was most relaxed. No matter how long. It might have barely lasted for a few seconds.

(i) Open your eyes now and be aware of your surroundings. Be grateful to your higher power, whether or not you had a desired experience in your meditation. I bow my head down with reverence, at this time, before a framed picture of a saint in my meditation room.

Your practice ends here. Enter now the world of your daily duties and meet them with the best positive attitude possible.

Summary

While meditating on music do not get your mind caught into analyzing the music, its flow, pitches, instruments played and intermittent pauses. As soon as you discover that your mind has gone focused out, gently lead it back to music. Do not fight or struggle with you mind when it wavers from its focus. This simply counteracts the purpose of your meditation. Let all your thought processes and physical presence gradually dissolve into the influence of the music. What makes this method popular and effective, compared to the other ones, is probably its convenience of carrying the music wherever one desires to, and replaying it for reinforcement time after time.

- - - - - - - - - -

Highlights Of
Meditation On Music

(1) Music has been woven into the tapestry of our lives at every stage for eons, from its conceptual stage through its final stage of death. Those who are aware of it have discovered ways to manage their moods, temperaments and stress in their lives better than others.

(2) Nature is the mother of all human composed music. Seize every opportunity possible to meditate when you are in the company of Nature. If your mind is receptive, you will experience something profound deep within.

(3) When selecting music, first listen to it for a couple of times, preferably with your eyes closed, at least a portion of it. Make your decision by the level of its influence experienced. *Feel* **the music rather than just listening.**

(4) Whenever your mind wavers lead it gently back to its focus. Combating with the distracting forces simply delays your progress. Learn to acknowledge them, and yet, not getting overpowered by them.

(5) Music is my mental getaway from my restless mind and continual demands of my life, to the gateway to my inner world of peace, joy and lights. It relaxes my mind and offers me an altered perception to see the same world better.

(6) Music has the power to influence your thoughts more than words, and your body's metabolism more than physician's prescriptions. Let the cells of your body and mind imbibe the music. Fully surrendering yourself to the waves of the music around you is the only way to deeply experience the state of relaxation.

= = = = = = = = = =

MEDITATION ON THOUGHTS

"With our thoughts we make our future,
with our thoughts we change our world."
(The Buddha)

Introduction

Thus far, we have discussed the methods of meditation on breathing and music. Now, we discuss the third method, meditation on our thoughts. We witness our thoughts arise and subside, emerge and fade, proliferating and battling among themselves over their importance. In all the four methods of meditation that I teach, my participants have found this one most baffling. They have often complained about this method being the most difficult one. The very concept of meditating on thoughts sounds self-contradictory to them.

Some participants, at times, have expressed their concern in these words, "Is it not what we do all day, thinking on one topic or another from the hour we wake up through the hour we go to sleep? If that is meditation in itself, what is the purpose of this method?" They also wondered, "How strange that on one hand you ask us to go beyond our thoughts to relax, and on the other hand, you ask us to focus on our very thoughts? If the thinking mind is to be ignored at all, how do we meditate without the mind at all? What do we focus on when the thoughts do not exist anymore?"

I can understand why the whole notion of "the mind watching the mind" seems to be so difficult to comprehend. I can relate to this dilemma very well. I used to experience the same dilemma when I was trying to learn this method, from books and people, in my early years of practice. Although I was often confused myself of my progress, I remained persistent in my practice.

I believed that if this technique has worked in the lives of others, it must work in mine too, unless I am following the instructions incorrectly, or this method is quite unsuitable to my natural mental proclivity. With time, my struggle subsided and a better understanding of the method dawned upon me. I endeavor here to translate my experiences, during my early periods of struggle and thereafter, hoping the same may benefit you.

Know that there is a subtle difference between our act of thinking thoughts, and the act of simply watching them. Though both acts focus on thoughts, in a sense, one, is basically a mechanical, subconscious process and the other is a planned out, conscious activity of our mind; one is a habitual process, the other is a disciplined process of our mind. The two different acts are taking place in the same mind, but in different domains. In the act of thinking, we participate as the players, whereas in the act of watching, we refuse to be players, and stand aside only observing the play objectively. Do you see the difference?

By the time you begin practicing this method of meditation, I would like you to realize, no matter how vaguely, that **you and your mental process are two separate entities.** We may, at times, be identifying ourselves with our minds' activities, but in essence, the mind and its owner are not the same. You as an owner possess the power to mold, shape and influence your mind, like an animal trainer in a circus. As you read further, it will become clearer to you.

The more we study the mechanism of our mind, the better we are in a position to employ its powers to our benefits. The more we examine our mind's modus operandi, the more we discover its possibilities and frailties. The more objectively we observe our mind's thought processes, which is the focus of this method, the higher we rise in our consciousness and deeper we experience the relaxed state.

In meditation on thoughts our mind is more inclined to be violent and chaotic compared to other methods. It is as if someone observing us makes us self-conscious and defensive for no apparent reasons. Therefore, whenever you find your thoughts getting turbulent in your meditation, take it naturally and non-judgmentally. The secret to success in this method is to focus on your thoughts and yet, remain uninfluenced by them.

When you focus on your thoughts, simply watch them nonchalantly. Do not judge them as good or bad, or right or wrong. Observe them like a busy traveler in haste, deeply engaged into the only thought of reaching his destination and oblivious to the hubbub of the environment around him. In a sense, fully aware of all that is going on around him, and yet, our busy traveler is mentally detached from them all.

The purpose of watching our thoughts is to transcend them through our personal indifference. If we feed our attention, knowingly or unknowingly, to our mind's tendencies of analyzing and judging, we never succeed meeting our goal of attaining a state of mental relaxation.

Focus on your thoughts but do not attempt to

control or modify them. An illustration from my childhood years may prove appropriate here. While growing up in a small village in India, we were used to be given a safety tip by wise people, which was, not to pay attention to the barking street-dogs when encountered; if unheeded and unprovoked, they will calm down and go away. This is the way to respond to our thoughts in meditation, and this is how I could progress in my practice.

Another tip to make your thoughts powerless is to keep them carefully uninfluenced by your emotions. **Thoughts draw their energy only on the level of attention given to them.** Thoughts when mixed with emotions grow more adamant, making us more restless. In meditation, when a thought of your workplace arises, for example, let it come, and try to watch it objectively. The moment you allow it to generate emotions in you such as of happiness, sadness, contempt or resentment, the thought gets a boost to proliferate.

Emotions are like the air in water-bubbles, drawing their very existence on the air within them. Similarly, our emotions are like the air in our thought-balloons. So long you disallow mixing emotions to your rising thoughts you are on the right focus in your meditation. This sense of awareness of your thoughts and emotions forms an important step to make effective of your practice in this method. With time and your growing awareness, you will naturally be able to keep your emotions away from mixing with your thoughts. This stage is not impossible to attain, but when attained, even to a trivial success, it will further help you in other areas of your life. You will not then take the unwarranted comments and hostile attitudes of others directed to you as you did before.

Few Common Examples

When a thought arises, say of the social party you had recently attended, forcing your mind in meditation to waver, this is how you probably can manage your composure. Obviously, this thought will naturally bring with it an army of the related thoughts. They may be, for examples, of the delicious dishes you had enjoyed, the new dress you wore, the compliments you had received on your look or attire, and the new friends you made that evening.

These thoughts, if you mix with the corresponding emotions such as of happiness and sadness, you are instigating your mind to freely roam away from its focal point. This often happens unknowingly. If you are alert instead, in preventing your emotions to arise, your thoughts will subside on their own after making some commotion in the beginning. With your rising alertness, you will be able to naturally separate them, and experience progress in your discipline.

During a session of meditation, a thought of the fluctuating stock market must not make you anxiety-ridden, nor a thought of a relative's illness must make you panic-stricken. A thought of an upcoming romantic evening must not drag you into a wild fantasy, nor a thought of a loss of a business deal must depress you. **Meditation is a discipline of raising our awareness, and developing personal indifference over the factors counteractive to our pursuit.** Some of you may still be saying to yourselves, "Easier said than done."

Allow me to present some living testimonials from our daily encounters. Let us take examples of physicians, surgeons, nurses, police officers, firefighters, and particularly of our 911-attendants. All in-coming calls, responded to by the 911-attendants are related to those seeking urgent aid in pain, torture, suffering and life threatening encounters. These attendants, though sensitive to the callers' pains, have trained their minds to rise above the influence of their personal feelings. If they keep identifying themselves with the pain and suffering of every caller, they cannot discharge their duties fully.

When on duty, they must remain self-composed and focused to their commitment of doing all within their power to guide and console the callers. They may themselves be ideal parents, siblings and friends outside the realm of their work, but when at work their emotions are regulated more by the rationale expected by their positions. Do you see how effortlessly they separate, at times, their minds from their hearts?

I share here my personal anecdote with an emergency room physician in a hospital. My father suffered a fall while crossing the road and was admitted to the emergency room of a nearby hospital. To take away my disturbed mind off his bleeding face, I initiated a conversation with the attending physician who was cleaning and stitching the open wounds around my father's nose.

I asked the physician, "Doctor, were you offered, during your medical schooling, some sort of training to desensitize your feelings when dealing with the patients' blood, wounds and pains?" She said, "No, though there should be some. The very nature of our job trains us to temporarily detach ourselves from the patients' feelings. We are not immune to patients' suffering. We simply act impersonal," the doctor later added. What a revealing approach!

This is what I suggest. Demonstrate personal indifference with your thoughts in meditation. If the phrase 'personal indifference' sounds negative to you, use 'impersonal' or 'detached' instead. Nevertheless, the meaning is the same—A temporary detachment at will.

Steps to Practice

It may help you to review the Chapter three, "The Seven Important Tips." It will reinforce the knowledge of the tips and help you better understand the following steps:

(a) Do the warm-up exercise: stretching and breathing.

(b) Choose your surroundings carefully. Prefer a quieter environment.

(c) Sit comfortably to uphold your focus longer and steadier.

(d) Set your timer to remind you to end your practice after about fifteen minutes.

(e) Begin your practice with a positive attitude. Raise your mind, for the duration of your practice at least, above its usual state of doubting and worrying.

(f) Close your eyes. Lead your attention gently at the point between your eyebrows and focus on your breaths. Now, begin slowly to count your exhalation, from one through fifteen. Watch your breath going in and going out. When it goes out count one. After inhaling again, when it goes out count two. Thus continue your normal breathing process and counting, adding one to your count every time your breathe out. When your mind wavers, bring it back to your breathing process and resume your counting.

(g) After you finish counting 15 exhalations, pay no more attention to your breathing, holding still your mental focus at the same spot, between your closed eyes. Know that your focus in this method remains, as steadfastly as possible, at the spot between your eyes throughout your practice. This will encourage you to practice with more awareness.

Be aware of your thoughts only. If you observe them through your 'third eye,' as referred in the Bible, located at the center between your eyes, you will be able to transcend the influence of your thoughts more effortlessly. Those who try to focus on the state of thoughtlessness instead often find themselves disappointed with the result. Know the difference between the witnessing and focusing. Whenever your mind wavers or drops in a slumber, gently lead it back to the point between your closed eyes with a sense of awareness of the rising, changing and subsiding thoughts. Continue this step till your timer goes off.

After your alarm goes off:

(h) Keep your eyes closed and relive, for a moment or two, the crescendo effect of relaxation you just experienced in your meditation. This experience may have lasted barely for a few seconds, which is common to those who are new to meditation. It could also be possible that you might not have any positive experience at all. Even veteran practioners have such sessions at times. Do not be over concerned for not having the desired experience.

(i) Release your focus from the center of your eyes and let it settle naturally. Open your eyes now, and be grateful to your higher power, whether or not you had experienced relaxed mind. At the end of my meditation, I bow my head before a framed picture of the saint of my high reverence.

Your practice ends here. Enter now the world of your daily duties and deal with it as composed and positive as possible.

Summary

Watch your thoughts as impersonally as possible, with no deliberate efforts to entertain them. Let the thoughts arise and take over your mental state. You simply watch with no personal interest, and you will find them soon gone, like the noise in a courtroom gradually subsides upon arriving of the judge.

The key of mastering this method is to carefully separate the arising thoughts from their corresponding emotions—a simple secret to easily attaining the state of mental relaxation. If you have such an experience even for a moment, know that you have touched a landmark in your progress. This method is not of struggles and fights against our wavering mind, but of recognizing the nature of our mind, and continually leading it back to the center between our closed eyes with no judgmental or reprimanding attitude to our mind.

Based on my experience, I caution you not to expect mastery over your thoughts in just few days; it takes time. This practice will make you further recognize the presence of another part of your mind, known as the higher mind or conscience, more powerful than your conscious, thinking mind, rendering to our thoughts a sense of clarity, and to our life a sense of direction.

- - - - - - - - - -

Highlights of
Meditation On Thoughts

(1) Thoughts in an undisciplined mind are like the monkeys, ever impatient and uneasy. Simply "witnessing" them nonchalantly will make them go away, like an unattended visitor. Until we transcend our restless mind, we cannot recognize its powers, realize its potentials, and take charge of our lives fully.

(2) As in a glass just filled with soiled water, the floating dirt particles slowly settle at bottom, leaving behind the water at top calmer and cleaner than before, similarly, as you uphold your focus on your thoughts, simply watching with awareness, you will experience your thoughts settling down leaving behind a state of mental serenity.

(3) Holding your focus at the point between your closed eyes, called the *ajna chakra or* command center, is a secret, not known to many, to transcend the influence of thoughts easily.

(4) What your mind identifies with determines your levels of success and happiness. Our thoughts are both our strengths as well as weaknesses. The success of this method will empower you to tune in your focus on what you desire and to tune out those thoughts, which you think are undesirable and negative to your growth.

(5) When uneasy in meditation, remind yourself of the **"911" attendants**, medical staff of an operating room and firefighters in actions, fully engrossed into their call of duty over their personal emotions. This will encourage you to progress in your meditation, separating your thoughts and emotions.

(6) A major benefit of this method is that you will be able to demonstrate your mental composure even in the midst of the hostile behaviors and demeaning comments of others at work, on the road and in relationships.

= = = = = = = = = =

MEDITATION ON *MANTRA*

"You know what you are, but
you do not know what you may be."
(Shakespeare)

Having discussed methods of meditation on our breathing, music and thoughts in the previous chapters, we now discuss the last method in our series, the *mantra*. What is a *mantra*? Is it the same as often translated as an affirmation? How does a mere repetition of few words alter us inside, or alter our mental state to relax? How can changing our outer behavior such as moving our lips in repeating an affirmation transform us from within?

Such questions naturally arise in the minds unfamiliar with the concept of the *mantra* or affirmation. In order to make this topic easier to comprehend, I have started this method with a brief discussion about an eastern concept of spiritual relationship, observed at times between a teacher and his disciples.

Teacher-Disciple Relationship

The word *mantra* comes from Sanskrit, a language widely used to communicate both in speaking and writing for many centuries in the ancient India, and thrives even today as a second language in academic institutes. *Mantra* is a compound word meaning 'what transcends or liberates a human mind'. As mentioned earlier in the book, meditation has a long history the East as discipline to know God. Paramahansa Yogananda puts it as a science of God-realization. For some people, finding God and living in Him is a self-accepted lifelong pursuit.

An enlightened teacher, the one who has attained himself the state of God realization, offers his students a *mantra* to facilitate their spiritual journey. A *mantra* is a syllable, word or a phrase. While granting a *mantra* the teacher also imparts a set of instructions for his students to observe when meditating on the *mantra*. A *mantra* may not be the same for all students because no two humans are identical. The teacher therefore carefully crafts a *mantra* and relevant instructions suitable to the needs, qualifications and mental disposition of each of his students. The teacher's only interest in granting a *mantra* to his students is enhancing their spiritual progress.

A relationship between a teacher and his students is believed to be God-ordained, honest and beyond material favors. The teacher's interest is the spiritual growth of his students, and the students' is an unconditional service and obedience to their teacher. A true teacher-disciple relationship is the purest among all relationships and is said to be, according to the esoteric science of the Hindus, coming from their previous lives. If you are interested to learn more about this relationship, I recommend you to read, *Autobiography of A Yogi*, particularly the chapter on "Years in My Master's Hermitage," which has deeply influenced my level of knowledge and growth.

The purpose of meditation is the same as that of prayers in all faiths: helping seekers transcend their material consciousness and recognize their human essence. A *mantra*, however, in a subtle sense is more than a word, endowed with the teacher's spiritual vibration. A *mantra* is a uniquely designed spiritual tablet impregnated with the teacher's blessings, which when meditated upon with faith and reverence for the teacher, possesses power to speed the students' progress faster than otherwise. The teacher's foremost instruction while offering a *mantra* is asking his students to focus on the visualized effect of the *mantra*, and not on the mere words. In that regard, a *mantra* is the same as an affirmation.

Self-Affirmation

The concept of self-affirmation in modern psychology has the same connotation and purpose as that of a *mantra*. In the West, we have not recognized the concept of a teacher-disciple relationship as in the East, but we have instead accepted the power of our own mind in place of a teacher. A self-affirmation substitutes the need of a teacher. A thoughtfully devised *mantra* by a teacher and a repetition of a well-crafted affirmation with awareness are effective in creating the desired influence in one's life. In this regard, an affirmation is the same as a *mantra* with however two minor differences. First, it is created by the practitioner himself or herself, and two, it can be modified, as and when needed, unlike the *mantra*, to suit one's changing needs.

This method of repeating an affirmation combines the power of mental concentration and faith in its operation. The practice of this method promises benefits in every phase of our lives—health, worldly success, relationships and spiritual evolution. An affirmation, aimed at one's personal growth, when repeated with awareness becomes autosuggestion.

While designing an affirmation, psychologists and self-help experts, warn against the use of negative terms. An affirmation must have positive words in it. I personally think differently. It is all right to occasionally use the seemingly negative words so long as the core and tone of the affirmation remain positive, and we do not get hung up on its negative aspect.

Sometimes, the negative words in a statement imply more positive force compared to using the positive words. Perhaps, this illustration will help you, "I shall not lose my composure today at workplace no matter how hard a situation may provoke me." Although the use of a negative word in this sentence, it gave me a positive impact while practicing meditation on affirmation at one stage in my personal life.

Because a spoken affirmation possesses the powers of our thoughts, words and concentration compared to a mental affirmation alone, it is highly recommended to beginner practitioners. This helps them to keep their focus steady. With time, as they grow accustomed to their practice, their lip-movement will naturally merge into their mental affirmation.

The following text sheds light on how a change in our words and pattern of thinking may influence a lasting change in our lives.

Power of Our Thoughts and Words

A practice of an oft-repeated affirmation, with a focus on its effect, is a powerful tool to unlock our minds' potentials. An affirmation when used for a positive effect becomes a positive affirmation. An affirmation, positive or negative, creates a corresponding effect, in lives of our own or of others. An affirmation alters our state of mind, a more effective source to improve the quality of our health compared to medical prescriptions.

Health practitioners declare that the pattern of our thoughts determine the nature of our health. When we are happy our body cells feel rejuvenated. When we are unhappy and stressful, our body cells feel dull and sluggish in vitality. When our mind is restless for any reason our health immediately responds, showing a disorder. We also know that the negative stress in our lives invariably aggravates the existing diseases and pains such as arthritis and ulcers. When our life at the workplace seems to be lacking interest and challenges, our body experiences dullness and fatigue.

On the other hand, when we are engaged in preparing for a long awaited family vacation or reunion, our body may not show the signs of fatigue, which otherwise would not be able to withstand such exertion. We observe such interactions between our mind and health in our daily life, but often we fail to identify the influence of our mind on our health. Our very mind is both the cause as well as the cure of most disorders in our health. By altering our attitude, we not only can prevent and cure the diseases in our health, we also can boost its natural immunity.

Those who recognize such stupendous power of our minds behind our overall success are the exponents of positive thinking. They declare that the nature of **our mental attitude is everything**. A positive attitude not only generates profound effects on our health, but in realms of our worldly achievements such as academic pursuits and relationships. Our level of success in meeting new challenges and maintaining a relationship are mostly based on our positive attitude toward our life.

Our attitude is more powerful than the strength of our personal resolves and influences of environment.

The advocates of the positive thinking movement like Dale Carnegie, Rev. Norman Vincent Peale and Napoleon Hill have immensely influenced our minds in past few decades. Dale Carnegie's book, *How To Win Friends and Influence People* is said to be one of the three books, after the Bible and Webster's Dictionary, most published and used in the United States. These thinkers maintain that thinking ourselves being healthy keep us healthy, and contrary to it is equally true. Our attitude is the most determining factor of our good or ill health, success or failure, happiness or miseries, rise or fall.

You may be wondering about my emphasis of attitude in this chapter. There is a direct influence of a right attitude in attaining the desired effect of this method of meditation, more than others. An affirmation is a reinforcement of our attitude, direct and effective beyond what an average mind can conceive.

When children are repeatedly reminded of their good conduct and achievements, no matter how trifling, over their flaws and failures, they are likely to demonstrate progress in their lives more than otherwise. When young adults are reminded of their dreams and visions over their areas of weaknesses and inabilities, they are more likely to shine out than otherwise. That is why the great ones often remind us to associate ourselves only with those who remind us of *what we can become*, and not *what we are*. Briefly, this method is about the power of words, the heard or spoken, and how we seriously we take them. **Eleanor Roosevelt** said: "No one can insult you unless you accept it."

Contrarily, when employees are reminded of their possibilities, instead of the past instances of their errors and poor performance, they are likely to perform better and show more initiatives than before. These are some of the common encounters, showing the powers of affirmations working subtly and effectively in our daily

life. A carefully selected word or words is the life-force
of an affirmation. The better the affirmation is crafted,
the more effectively it works. I have tried to further
explain below how the spoken words influence us
inside, penetrating our subconscious mind.

Power of Our Subconscious Mind

The words we hear or read create an immediate
corresponding impression in our conscious mind, and
the same words, when repeated several times, create
an impression deeper evermore in what is known as
our subconscious mind. This impression may be
forgotten with time, but is never erased. That is why
our subconscious mind is much more influencial
compared to our conscious mind, in shaping our future
and destiny. Our conscious mind may not be able to
recollect someone's name, phone number or a birth date,
although we might have heard it just a few minutes
before or several times in the past, but it is carefully
retained by our mind deep in its recesses. This is how
our subconscious mind operates.

The major contents of our subconscious mind
determine our level of overall growth, in health, success
at work and in relationships. That is why we hear the
wise people always advising not to take to heart the
evil words and comments intended to belittle us lest
they find a niche in our mind. Delving in negative
impressions of our own thoughts or of the words
uttered by others has a great influence in our lives. Our
conscious mind may forget the negative impressions,
sooner or later, but our subconscious mind never drops
anything off its system, be it good or evil.

With regard to how our thoughts and their
impressions left behind influence in shaping our entire
life, we may find in the following lines.

Mahatma Gandhi is quoted to say this:

Watch your thoughts, because
 your thoughts will become your words;

Watch your words, because
 your words will become your actions;

Watch your actions, because
 your actions will become your habits;

Watch your habits, because
 your habits will become your attitude;

Watch your attitude, because
 your attitude will become your values;

Watch your values, because
 your values will become your character;

Watch your character, because
 your character will make your destiny.

The following incident may best illustrate the power of our subconscious mind. It is a true story from the life of Bonnie, one of my seminar participants. Her situation may relate to you all in one way or another.

Bennie's Personal Predicament

Whatever our conscious mind finds is undesirable or painful, it tries to discard it at once from its domain, but it is not totally flushed out of our system. This experience is instantly captured by our mind's subconscious part where it seeks its shelter permanently until efforts are made to erase it. That is why the origins of deep-rooted traumas, guilt, chronic habits and phobias are not easily diagnosed. Only skilled psychiatrists or hypno-therapists can ably diagnose their causes by placing their patients in an altered state of consciousness such as a hypnotic trance to further penetrate the layers of their subconscious mind.

In some instances, this process is called 'age regression'. The negative influences of our past experiences held by our subconscious mind often impede our growth and progress, at times even decades later. I think this is what had occurred in the life of Bonnie, a young participant in one of my seminars, whom I recommended this method, meditation on affirmation.

Bonnie, a young student in one of my seminars on maintaining Positive Attitude shared the following: Whenever she went for a job interview, a doubt seized her mind that she was not going to get the position. Though she was fully assured, based on her credentials and background, that she was a perfect candidate for the announced job, and on some occasions, she had been already pre-qualified for the position by the prospective employers on the telephone, the sense of self-doubting would begin uncoiling and dominate her mind from the morning of the interview day.

Bonnie wondered herself why that skeptic attitude chased her all the time, particularly for the last few months. She had absolutely no idea of why it was happening to her, despite the fact that she normally possessed a high level of self-assertiveness. Evidently, some event of the past, profound and unpleasant, was blocking her progress.

To help her erase from her mental slate the negative effects of the unpleasant incident, I advised her to practice this method of meditation. She could also practice the technique of meditative visualization, discussed earlier in this book, under someone's guidance. Either of these psychological techniques is effective to alter the pattern of grooves in our subconscious mind created by some traumatic experience, the details of which are now conveniently dropped by our conscious mind.

The repetition of a thought creates a groove in our mind. This happens very subtly and precisely. This is how our mind forms habits and mental inhibitions such as self-doubting, phobias and inferiority complexes. One way to effectively change it is through exercising counter autosuggestions. This helps erase the negative impressions, no matter how deep and chronic, gradually altering our present attitude to more positive. This method of affirmation is a powerful tool to heal our impaired past, and make our future more rewarding. **William James**, a renowned American psychologist declared, "The greatest discovery of my generation is that human beings can alter their lives by altering their attitudes."

Let's now discuss about the steps of the method to make our meditation on affirmation more effective.

Steps to Practice

Reviewing again Chapter Three, "The Seven Important Tips," may help you. It will reinforce the knowledge of the tips to enable you better understand the steps, and absorb your mind more easily into your meditation.

(a) Do the warm-up exercise: stretching and breathing.

(b) Choose your surroundings carefully. Prefer a quieter environment.

(c) Sit comfortably to help you maintain your correct posture for a longer, steadier focus.

(d) Keep a carefully crafted affirmation possibly written, and place it in front of you at eye level to read easily, if needed.

The affirmation may read, for example, "I am relaxed," "I am at peace with myself," "I feel healthy, positive and self-composed," or "I shall accept gracefully anyone and anything that may cross my path today." A written affirmation may help you in case your mind wavers off its focus and gets turbulent. On these occasions, open your eyes, focus on the written affirmation and read it a couple of times. Then try again to focus on the visualized effect of it within your eyes closed. After a few days, your focus will grow steadier.

(e) Set your alarm clock to remind you to end your practice after about fifteen minutes.

(f) Begin your practice with a positive attitude. Raise your mind, at least for the duration of your practice, above its usual state of doubts and worries.

(g) Close your eyes. Lead your attention gently at the point between your eyebrows and focus on your breaths. Now, begin to count your exhalation one through fifteen. Watch your breath going in and going out. When it goes out count one. Thus continue your normal breathing process, adding one to your count every time you breathe out. When your mind wavers do not be discouraged. Lead it gently back to its focus.

(h) Now, shift your attention to the affirmation you wish to focus on. Repeat it a couple of times verbally, and then again mentally, slowly and rhythmically. Lead your focus now on the desired effect of the affirmation and "see" yourself in your visualized image.

If your affirmation is, "I am calm and composed," repeat it a few times outwardly as well as inwardly, and imagine yourself as though you are truly rested, refreshed and fully in charge of yourself at a given moment. Practice this affirmation with focus and no hurry. Pause for about thirty seconds before your next affirmation. This pause will encourage your mind to absorb its effect deeper and retain it longer than before. With time, this vision will sink further down into your mind, someday making it the very fabric of your nature. Continue till your alarm goes off.

After your alarm goes off:

(i) Release your focus from the center of your eyes and let it settle naturally. Relive, for a moment or two, again with your eyes closed, the peak experience your mind had enjoyed, no matter how long. It might have barely lasted for a few seconds.

(j) Open your eyes now and be aware of your surroundings. Be grateful to your higher power, whether or not you had a desired experience in your meditation. I bow my head down with reverence, at this time, before a framed picture of a saint in my meditation room.

Your practice ends here. Enter the world of your daily duties and meet them with the best possible attitude.

A Tip

Another way to practice this method is to use an audiocassette. I learned this technique from some of my students. You may record your affirmation, preferably in your own voice, onto an audiocassette, CD or a similar devise, repeated for ten to fifteen times, depending on the length of your affirmation and the time allocated for the practice. Remember to pause following each repetition. Then play it during your practice. After you feel comfortable with your practice, it maybe a good idea to recreate your audiocassette with a longer pause after each of your affirmation. Recorded affirmations will substitute your need for a timer, and encourage you to hold your focus longer.

Overcoming the Fight-or-Flight Syndrome

The following anecdote from my personal life may show you how this method of meditation came to my rescue when I was once facing a personal challenge at my workplace. Everything about the workplace seemed to be testing my patience and temperament—the commute, nature of work, associates and management. Within a couple of weeks after I landed this job, I discovered that I had unduly rushed in accepting the offer.

The nature of my job description turned out to be different than what I had understood when accepting the position. Obviously, as you probably could gather by now, it was a situation of fight or flight. I calmly weighed the pros and cons of the available options. Fighting the management is often not a wise idea, especially, for the new one on board, and flight was not practical either, in the interest of personal pride and survival. My intuition suggested to me a third option to the situation that the wise people advise at times—when your heart and mind do not harmoniously agree at some crucial moment in your life, wait till the situation changes itself; you do not force change it.

I determined to make the best of the situation in the interest of my personal growth, and turned within, with more sincerity, in meditation for the guidance. As blessed on several occasions in the past, I received a timely guidance, indicating me to alter my method of meditation. I gradually shifted my focus to affirmation.

I crafted thoughtfully on a piece of paper an appropriate affirmation, which as I recall today was of this nature:

"I must make the best of this situation in the interest of my personal growth. There must be some purpose for me to travel this road. I shall conduct myself at work, in gestures and thoughts, only in the way that may make me proud of myself at the end of the day. Help me, God!"

Besides meditating more faithfully on this affirmation every morning before leaving home, I used to repeat it at work, as well, before leaving my car, and also during my scheduled responsibilities whenever possible and needed.

The aforesaid affirmation may seem to be long to some of you. If you however see through it, you may feel a single tone loud and clear—I must adapt myself to seemingly unchangeable. **This technique of repeating affirmation with awareness would set the tone of my day,** and reprogram my mind, day after day, to accept the accountability for the situation and make it a challenge, turning it into my learning experience. The changed method of meditation immensely helped alter my attitude to manage better the circumstances.

This meditation on affirmation encouraged me to work thereafter with a greater sense of interest in the work and others. About a year later, a new position with greater challenges came my way. On reflection today, over the bygone period of my life, I feel proud of myself for having risen above the fight-or-flight predicament. It matured and prepared me for greater challenges in work as well other areas of my life.

I cited this personal encounter only to show you how, in certain situations, meditating on affirmations benefit us, and how it could be practiced for faster result. **Hitler** used to say that a lie, when repeated a thousand times, becomes a truth in itself. Hitler was probably aware of the power of affirmation, but he had exercised it in his vested interest. Some professional boxers also use this principle of psychology to break morale of their opponents in the ring. The same technique when used in a positive way can transform one's life. This technique of affirmation when practiced rightly possesses the power, not only to help improve our health, change habits, and attain our worldly pursuits, but also to transform our lives forever.

Summary

This method of meditation on affirmation works directly on the principle of the human mind that whatever vision it perpetually lives in, it eventually becomes. Whether a teacher-granted mantra or self-crafted affirmation, both possess the same power—making us what we desire to be. They reprogram our minds, subtly and profoundly, to make possible the desired effects in any area of our lives, which could be of improving health, increasing or reducing weight, breaking or forming habits, attaining success, or speeding our spiritual progress.

The secret to the success of this practice, like in other meditative practices, lies in how well we focus on the visualized effect of our affirmation, and not merely on its mechanical repetition. Exercise this technique, outside your usual session of meditation, whenever and wherever you can to make materialize the desired change faster in your life.

Highlights of
Meditation on 'Mantra'

(1) The word *mantra* means that which transcends or liberates our mind. It often acts as a spiritual bond between an enlightened teacher and his disciples.

(2) A *mantra* is granted to the students according to their level of attitude developed and mental propensities. In a same token, design your affirmation yourself suitable to the demand of the situation at a given period in your life. .

(3) An affirmation is a self-designed word or phrase, which when repeated with a sense of concentration and awareness, works as a well-aimed bullet, forcing the desired result to materialize. It has a power to heal our damaged past, change our habits and shape our destiny.

(4) Every affirmation, through creating a corresponding image in our mind, changes our mental attitude whether good or bad. Therefore, be careful about the nature of your affirmation.

(5) When your affirmation is brief and repeated rhythmically with a pause in between, it will speed your journey.

(6) The beauty of this method is that you can modify your affirmation as often as you need to, and also carry it with you onto a cassette or CD wherever you go.

(7) This technique has been found by many immensely effective when placed in an unpleasant situation, and no alternative seems to be practical—to redeem from the predicament faster than otherwise.

= = = = = = =

Some of My Favorite Affirmations

(1) I have no need to worry because my Higher Power is always with me.

(2) I shall stay calm and self-composed no matter what may come.

(3) I am recovering and regaining my good health. My bodily and mental cells are rejuvenating every day, every hour of it. I am feeling better, and growing healthier and stronger evermore.

(4) I am the soul, eternal and ever peaceful. I therefore need not fear and worry. I am ever safe and secured in my Father's hands.

(5) Oh Heavenly Father, bless me that I may find myself in peace and happiness in place of worries and anxieties all the times.

(6) I will greet everyone crossing my path today, friends, foes and strangers alike, with smile and candidness. Oh Lord, help me judge no one.

(7) Oh Lord, train me today to cooperate with all events, pleasant or unpleasant, and help me to learn lessons out them. Give me courage to bear that I cannot change.

(8) I shall maintain my poise all day long, no matter how hard an event or individual may try to provoke me.

(9) Oh Divine, bless me with more strength, courage and wisdom to overcome all trials and tribulations of my life today.

These suggestions are only in a general interest.

You know your mental disposition and personal needs better than others. You may therefore craft your own affirmation, or modify any of the suggested ones here or elsewhere in this book, to suit your personality and needs. They possess power to better every situation in our lives. As much it helps us to succeed in every phase of our lives—health, worldly achievements and relationships—so much it helps us alleviate our fear, anxiety, worries and stress. It changes our way of thinking, temporarily or permanently, depending on our levels of interest and sincerity in our practice.

I have tested most of these affirmations, on several occasions, in my personal life and have found them highly beneficial. To learn more about the power of affirmations, I highly recommend two references, *METAPHYSICAL MEDITATIONS*, and *SCIENTIFIC HEALING AFFIRMATIONS*, both by Paramahansa Yogananda published by the Self Realization Fellowship, Los Angeles, California. I have personally found these booklets very beneficial.

- - - - - - - - - -

THE LIVING MEDITATION

"Do not do what you want,
and then you may do what you like."
(Sw. Sadashiv)

Living meditation means to live on into the desired effects of meditation even beyond the time allocated for meditative practice. It is to demonstrate the intended effect of the discipline in our interactions with the world through all means possible, our words, acts and even thoughts. One should strive to carry out the effect of the peace of mind attained during the practice of meditation in the morning, even while interacting with the traffic on the road, members in the family, and coworkers, superiors or subordinates at work. When the mental composure experienced during our meditation session begins pervading our behavior with others in our daily life is the state of living meditation.

Our day-to-day behavior with others must reflect our composure. In a sense, the result of our few minutes of meditation in the morning should gradually become an integral part of us. As our health and appearance reflect what we eat and drink, and our mental growth shows what influences our mind absorbs from our reading, thinking and interactions with the world, similarly our demeanor through out the day must naturally reflect the influence of our morning meditation. The following true anecdote from the life

of a saint and his disciple will illustrate what I intend
to say here.

Saint Namdev

There lived in India, a saint named Namdev. One
night, when on a routine round of supervision in his
disciples' lodgings, he noticed that one of his disciples
hastily hiding something under his bed-mat. On an
inquiry, the disciple apologetically admitted that he was
trying to hide a fruit that he had received in his alms.
Being ill, he knew that he would not be able to go out
again next day begging for alms. He was tempted
therefore to break the rules of the hermitage over his
possible starvation next day.

The teacher was deeply disappointed in his
student. He chastised the disciple: "My dear child, is it
what I have been teaching you all these years? Did
you forget the vow you had taken on the day of your
initiation that you would not possess materially beyond
your basic needs, and surrender yourself to the will of
God? You lost your faith so easily in the One who
nurtures the billions of His creatures in this vast
Existence including the little worms!

Seeing the tears in his *guru* and moved by his
words, the disciple fell at once at his teacher's feet and
implored for forgiveness. This experience transformed
the life of the disciple forever. He later became an
enlightened teacher himself and influenced the lives of
many. The teacher's emphasis was not the fruit as such,
but implementing a discipline in his students, which
may eventually become an integrated part of their way
of living. The teacher's interest was in helping his
students to anchor their consciousness to the faith in
God, more than in the petty material possession in their
lives.

A thinker once said that the purpose of education should not be limited to collecting the diplomas and attaining high positions at workplaces; it should make us better humans. This is what the saint Namdev was interested in, and what I mean by the living meditation. **With time, the effects of our discipline should blend into our very way of daily living.**

The ultimate purpose of every discipline, whether physical, mental, moral or spiritual, should be our personal enrichment. While working on a weight reduction program, for example, our interest should be in how best we may enjoy the improved quality of our health more than in how charming we may look. While working on improving our attitudes our interest should be in growing in our true success and relationships, more than in impressing others or temporary worldly achievement. Thus the purpose of meditation is to rise above the experience of mental relaxation during the practice, and maintain it throughout our interactions with others during the remainder of our day. It is a way to integrate, into the very fabric of our day-to-day life, the benefits of our daily meditation no matter how short lived.

I have presented below a scenario of a typical day from the life of Paul, a busy corporate executive. This hypothetical situation may prove equally true, to some degree, in your own life.

Can You Help Executive Paul?

Paul is a busy executive and generally remains engrossed. in his long work hours, six days a week. Though highly career oriented, he effectively manages his priorities between his career and family by spending Sundays with his family. Paul is professionally successful and a fine human being except that he lacks a sense of poise in his temperament. This lack of virtue deprives him of reaching the height of success he strives to attain. Paul's temper, hyper, anxiety ridden and often unpredictable, keeps his personal life tense. He cannot predict and control his own temper when provoked by a situation or other's behavior.

The level of his relationship with others, at his work as well as in the family, seems bumpy and superfluous at times despite his generosity and kind heartedness. What is most admirable in his nature is his habit of self-reflection. He later discovers his wrongdoings himself. He frankly admits his faults, and realizes the need for self-improvement. Having tried out several disciplines without much success, Paul finally turns to learning meditation.

Following the initial period of struggle to focus, Paul gradually begins to enjoy the state of relaxation. He dedicates few minutes daily to his morning practice before leaving home, and seems to be enjoying peace at the end of his practice. The desired effect in Paul's life, however, lasts only for a little while. As soon as he leaves his home, his mind gets restless over almost everything in the world.

On the road, Paul gets upset at the congested traffic, the "stop" signs and red lights, slow motorists before him and the changed weather condition. At work, he gets upset with the latecomers in the meetings, with his secretary over trivial issues, with his computer for its delayed responses, and with his peers for not returning his phone calls in a timely manner. On the way back home, his mind again passes through the same agitated state as it was in the morning, and finally, when he reaches home he finds himself physically tired and mentally exhausted, with no energy left to spend time with his family. Many good qualities in Paul have made him a successful executive, but he seems to be often at war with himself within.

It seems that there are two "Pauls" in one body, and both seem to be conflicting with each other. Paul feels happy with himself, peaceful and self-integrated, until he has left his home, but thereafter, he seems to have no control over himself. Once he is out amidst his life's daily battles, starting with the moment he leaves his home in the morning, he is no more the same. *The Paul* in meditation and *the Paul* facing the real world are two different entities, outwardly one, but inwardly opposites, the state that keeps him continually self-divided inwardly, and restless outwardly.

As I see, if Paul continues living with his present way, unchecked and uncorrected, he may simply devastate his life, jeopardizing all his relationships— with his work, family, friends and above all, with his own health. Our Paul, to an extent, represents all of us in one period of time or another in our lives. **Those who are disintegrated within are seldom able to touch the peaks of accomplishments, and enjoy their life to its fullest.** Those who are not happy with themselves cannot be naturally happy with others, too. "Those who cannot get along with themselves cannot get along with others," **Paramahansa Yogananda** declares. I think our Paul is in need of an urgent help.

What do you think seems to be happening in our Paul's life? Why does he seem to be a failure at the end of the day as opposed to his success in meditation before leaving home? Shouldn't the one meditating regularly be found content and composed? What do you think Paul seems to be missing in his daily life? What would you suggest to him who is gifted with many fine humanly qualities, but overly impatient; possesses a sense of discrimination between the right and wrong, but cannot live it himself most of the time; persistent in self-improvement, but lacking patience in dealing with the world; enjoying the benefit of meditation, but failing to carry it out into his practical life? What would you suggest to our Paul to bridge the apparent gap between his personalities? I advice you to pause here for a few minutes to examine our Paul's struggle before you continue. See if you have some suggestions for Paul.

My Suggestions to Paul

I might suggest to Paul the following. He needs something more than his daily meditation to retain his self-composure longer, the desired effect of his meditation. I have discovered three tools in my own life, each of which is highly influential to speed the progress of any discipline regardless of its nature and intent. Each tool is profoundly influential and promises the beginners as well as the experienced the results of their discipline in a time much shorter than otherwise. Let us see what they are and how they may profit our Paul.

The Three Power-Tools

(1) The Power of Reminder
(2) The Power of Environment
(3) The Power of Visualization

The Power of Reminder

Interestingly, I had learned about this tool from my mother when I was a child about eight year old. When on her weekly chore, she used to occasionally take me with her to the bazaar, a marketplace in our small town. I observed that, before leaving home, my mother at times would tie a knot at the hem of her *sari*, a long garment that most Hindu women customarily wear. It was a reminder to her of buying a particular item during her errand. After having ensured herself, on way back to home, that she had bought the particular item already, she would release the knot.

What took me years to understand the principle of association well, our forefathers seemed to have already known without undergoing formal schooling. The concept of the "knot" evolved later into the form of paper, and today, into an electronic form. This is what our Paul first must have, a "knot", a reminder to himself, for few weeks at least besides his daily practice of meditation, to help his mind anchor into the state of self-composure, which at present is restricted only to the duration of his morning meditation.

My Personal Challenge Once At Workplace

An anecdote once from my personal life may further demonstrate the influence of this power, the power of a reminder. Though quoted in one of the earlier chapters of this book already, this personal experience of mine may better illustrate my point. I have repeated it here in a different tone and style compared to way mentioned before.

Some years ago I was caught into a situation of working with an unfriendly coworker. By nature, she was tense, irritable and a gossipmonger. She would make every new employee in her department a target of her gossip with some of our coworkers. Now, it was my turn. With time, as our coworkers became close to me, they would privately share with me what she had whispered about me into their ears. "What an abusive way of utilizing company's time and god-given abilities to think and speak!"—I would say to myself.

It was difficult for me not to think of her offensive

behavior and focus on my work at the same time. My attempts to privately reason with her had failed. Bringing my predicament to the attention of our supervisor or confronting her openly seemed to be the only alternatives, and yet neither was practical to me. The first was not advisable to a new employee, and the other was not suitable to my temperament. The pressing dilemma forced me to explore a third alternative.

I had learned that she was good at heart. She was a high achiever in her position and possessed many noble qualities as a wife, mother and grandmother. It was only at work that her behavior was different and undesirable to many around, which seemed to be an outward expression of something else troubling her deep down beyond her own knowledge. This analysis gave me a hope to befriend her someday. I resolved to forbear.

Whenever I found the situation exhausting my funds of forbearance, I would draw my strength from the "knot" in the form of a written reminder to myself that I had placed conspicuously on my desk. Whenever her behavior would make me restless, I would turn to my written reminder, which always encouraged me to "bear a little more" and refrain me from demonstrating an impulsive behavior. Like a beacon, the reminder helped me on several instances to retain my sanity and remain self-composed during the aggravated moments. As I recall today years later, the reminder was in the following words: "I shall not lose my self-composure no matter how hard the situation may provoke. If my mind is *mine*, it should be in my control, and not in other's."

Never receiving the expected response from my nonchalant attitude, her behavior toward me began gradually mellowing down. She began picking up opportunities to communicate with me more positively. With time, we began understanding each other better and became good colleagues. When I resigned from the company, she actively participated in organizing a farewell party in my honor. I am happy to admit today that my early period of working with her offered me a rare challenge to test and demonstrate my long meditative practice.

It turned out to be my life-enriching experience, and in a sense hers too. I was the first one in her many years of work-life who had reacted to her with such a sense of respect professionally, and yet, with a sense of indifference personally. I had never wished her ill, nor condemned my situation then. I was carefully focused to making the best of the circumstance in my personal growth. I share here with you this personal anecdote only to show you how profound and effective is the influence of a reminder when used with awareness.

This is what our Paul needs, a "knot," to frequently remind himself, to stay calmer and take it easier, a profoundly effective way to help change oneself. He may keep the reminder in his pocket, on the dashboard of his car or on his desk at work as one may find me practicing even today. He may employ his own ingenuity to discover a "knot" as a friend of mine, Tim, once had discovered at one stage in his own life. Tim used to carry in his key-chain a wooden statuette of three little monkeys, sitting side by side, one with his hands on his mouth, the other on his ears, and the third on his eyes. You may have seen this popular Chinese statue whose timeless message is obvious and poignant: Do not see, speak and hear what is not conducive to your growth. It immensely helped Tim to dissuade himself from the company of unworthy friends and unhealthy habits. Such is the power a reminder when used with heightened sense of perception.

The "Knots" In Diverse Faiths

We find reminders, in varied forms, practiced in all faiths. The ultimate purpose of human journey in every major faith is spiritual evolution, which is embedded with many turns, challenges and temptations. One without proper direction is apt to get lost onto this path. Our wise ancestors have therefore interwoven reminders in the form of rituals onto this transformational journey of our lives. They are like the highway signs to interstate motorists.

The wearing of the cross around necks, placing family pictures on our office desks and placing dots in the foreheads by married women in a certain faith are some of the reminders to us. They are suggested to us in varied forms such as metal idols, statues, rosaries, religious rituals and pictures of deities. They encourage us, time after time, to stay focused and disciplined. They reinforce our faith. They stimulate in us a sense of hope and direction, of joy and comfort, of faith and security. Let us look into the illustrations in different faiths.

The mental state of a Hindu changes naturally when he is passing by a temple of his faith. His heart fills up at once with devotion and reverence. The same happens to a Christian when passing by his church, and to a Muslim when passing by his mosque. The sight of a place of worship stirs something in our deepest core. It invokes in us a sense of reverence, devotion and humility; a sense of our identity, which often lies buried under the layers of our material consciousness and myriad demands of our daily busy life.

The married Hindu women wearing dots on their foreheads, the Hindu swamis and Buddhist monks wearing orchard clothes, the Hindu devotees prostrating before deities in their temples or domestic shrines, the Christians falling on their knees in their churches, and the devotees in certain faiths taking their shoes off before entering their prayer houses are some of the reminders to us in our daily lives, instituted by our prophets and spiritual masters. **These reminders in the form of rituals, when followed with awareness of their significance, help reinforce our faith, and speed the progress of our discipline irrespective of its nature.**

During my early years of meditation, I used to close my room while meditating for more than the reason of preventing the outside noise. The purpose of it was more a psychological one, reminding myself that my outside world with its myriad problems, demands and clamors was symbolically shut out. I must admit that it profoundly helped me.

The use of external aids such as candles, incense, cymbals and gong bells in worship houses are only the reminders to help devotees sustain their focus and enhance the desired effects of their practice. Once our mind gets grounded to the discipline, the need of reminders becomes redundant. Nevertheless, they are profoundly beneficial, particularly in the beginning of our journey, till our discipline becomes a part of our daily life.

Similarly, our Paul's focus on his reminder will encourage him to manage his restless temper and sustain his self-composure. In a sense, it is more than a focus. In the process of focusing, there still exist two: The mind and the object of focus. As our focus deepens with time, the duality drops, and the purpose of focus becomes a part of our nature. Until such a mental state is reached where Paul can demonstrate poise even against the seemingly hostile factors around him, he must always carry with him a reminder in a tangible form.

(2) *The Power of Environment*

Often, the power of environment is stronger than our personal resolve. The adverse weather and prying eyes of the wayward animals are more influential on a tender plant than its own potential to grow. We need therefore to be selective of our environment, particularly when we are new to our discipline. We must associate ourselves more with only those friends, co-workers, places and books whose presence and words encourage us.

The outside environment that fails to awaken our potentials and abilities is not a right environment for us. It is that simple. We must try to move out of it. Choose friends who might not be pleasant and polite with you always, but keep your well-being and growth close to their hearts. This is what our Paul needs to be aware of. Perhaps, a true example from the life of Jackie may illustrate the power of this tool.

Jackie Finally Quits Smoking

Jackie, one of my ex-colleagues, attained a major accomplishment in her life. She could quit her chronic habit of smoking cigarettes. She probably had intuitively realized the power of environment, having a group of supportive friends around her. She began associating herself with few select peers, and candidly sought their support in her battle. We began helping her in this way.

Whenever an urge to smoke possessed her, one of us would deviate her from leaving the building to go out and smoke. We would take her to the in-house cafeteria, and buy her a cup of tea, coffee or hot chocolate instead. After a couple of weeks, her smoking was reduced to almost half compared to her earlier consumption. Jackie was cooperating with us. She knew well that this was happening in her own interest. Above her own resolve, she needed some timely encouragement from those whom she trusted. After about six weeks or so, she limited her smoking to only three cigarettes for the day, and after two more weeks, she quit smoking entirely.

A gesture of few encouraging words from others impacts our progress more positively and effectively than our own determination by itself. **Our fellowship with others often plays a determining role in shaping our future and making our destiny.** The kind of friends we associate ourselves with possesses the power to make or break our future. The wise parents know this well, which is why they caution their children against playing with some of their peers, and encourage playing with others. The right company can save us from falling, and helps accelerate our progress.

This is what our Paul needs to realize, the power of environment in his life, and encourage himself to associate only with that which supports his resolve to meet his challenge. Joining a like-minded group has an added influence on us, positive, penetrative and effective. If Paul is an introvert and reserved by temperament, he may decide to focus, rather than seeking new friends, on selecting the right books, habits and movies. Paul may also exercise his reasoning in watching movies and television-shows, and disregarding the ones that do not help him calm his mind against the influence of the provocative forces in his daily life. He should select only such music that may help him manage his hyper-anxiety ridden nature.

In my personal life, I have realized the profound impact of books, more than any other factor. Inspirational books never fail us. The best way to read a book is to introspect about it. See how it applies to us personally. We need not accept and absorb all that is printed in the book. Paul should therefore accept in books only what passes the test of his intelligence and intuitive insight. If the book inspires him to think and grow, that may prove to him more influential than his all good friends combined.

A scriptural reading may prove to Paul the best source to calm his temper and keep him focused. A busy executive of a known corporation had a habit of referring to the Proverbs whenever mentally restless at his work. The message given to our mind before our bedtime leaves a lasting effect, and sets the tone for a good night's sleep as well as for the next morning.

The food we eat, friends and coworkers we associate with, and the hobbies, habits and the activities we engage ourselves in combined forms our environment. We do not always have control over the environment. There is both the good and ugly around us, because it is the very nature of our world. Paul therefore must exercise his discriminatory sense in choosing only that which is homogenous to the purpose of his discipline. He should spare some time to regularly read what is inspirational and comforting to his usually agitated temperament, particularly before going to sleep when the mind is more receptive. These are my general recommendations to our Paul.

(3) *The Power of Visualization*

This tool is a modified version of the technique, Meditative Visualization, discussed in the beginning of this book. Nevertheless, they both operate under the same psychological principle. I have discussed this technique here with some length again for two reasons. One, to reinforce the same principle, and two, it is much modified to help out Paul with his problem. In a sense, this discussion will help you too, whenever the 'little restless Paul' within you ever gets difficult to manage.

Our mind is the ultimate influential factor in making our present, molding our future and shaping our future. Besides selecting a right focus in meditation, what is further important is to continually delve into it. If you recall, I have emphasized, in each of the four methods of meditation discussed in Section II earlier, on recalling the climatic state of relaxation experienced in your meditation session and again reliving it, for a moment or two before your practice ends. Our level of progress in life depends on the nature of thoughts we feed to our mind. Even what we continually think during our quiet, free moments, determines our over all success, subtly and effectively. Our present tool, the power of visualization operates on this very principle.

I have often reminded you to relive the peak experience you had in your meditation, as frequently as possible, during the rest of the day no matter how busy you are. If you cannot succeed in bringing that experience to your mind for some reason, you may alternatively remind yourself the purpose of your meditative practice and hold your mind onto it as long as you can. The following analogies may further help you to understand my point.

When exhausted in an arduous endeavor of climbing a mountain, resting for a while and visualizing of having already reached the summit renders the climbers a positive feeling and revitalizes their level of enthusiasm. A painter, while using his brush on the canvas, holds in his mind the final picture of his painting. A sculptor, each time strikes his hammer on the chisel, holds in his mind the final form of his statue. A professional runner, when on the track, envisions himself or herself crossing the finish line first.

These are the few examples from our daily lives

where a trained and resolved mind exercises visualization often unknowingly. This is what our Paul needs to be reminded of. No matter how busy with his daily preoccupations, he must spare a few minutes, now and then, to visualize himself experiencing peace, calmness, and self-composure.

While trying out a new outfit in front of a full sized mirror in a shop, we picture ourselves at that instant standing dressed up before an imagined audience. Though, in a sense, it is merely an imagination of our mind, it actually stirs and invokes something within us at that moment. Our visualized state, though contrary to the reality at a given moment, influences our decision to buy. In a similar way, it works in different phases of our lives, eventually speeding our progress subtly and unfailingly.

This mental process of visualization works on a simple psychological principle that the nature of our dominant thoughts produces the corresponding effects on our physical state. While thinking about some pleasant events of the past, we not only experience ourselves being happy, uplifted and exalted, but it also promotes our health through positively influencing its physical cells. Conversely, while thinking about some traumatic experience of the past, or worrying over the condition of our dear one in the hospital, makes us sad and helpless. This negatively impacts our health making it more vulnerable to diseases. This medically proven interaction between our mind and its physical counterpart, our health, is called psychosomatic.

My interest in discussing this topic at this length and at times repeating some points is only to remind you of the profound influence of our mental attitude in our health and other areas of our lives. **The thoughts of** *"what we can become"* **have more power in shaping our destiny than the thoughts of** *"what we are."* What we perpetually think, so do we eventually become. **William James,** an eminent psychologist, observed, "The greatest discovery of my generation is that human beings, by changing the inner attitude of their minds, can change outer aspects of their lives."

Paul may carefully orchestrate, as often as possible during the rest of his day, living in the vision of the "new Paul," the image of how he wishes to see himself changed. Withdrawing himself to some quiet place for a few minutes, Paul may close his eyes and envision himself as though he is calm and composed in his response to the people and events. Thus he focuses on the desired change, the temperamental calmness and inner harmony, and not on his present state of restlessness and inner struggles. This impression about himself conjured up in his visualization will subtly influence his behavior and help him realize someday what he desires to be.

Summary

The living meditation is the state when the difference between our desired mental attitude and its corresponding outward behavior completely drops, as we saw in saint Namdev. When we begin demonstrating ourselves as calm and poised while interacting with others, we are said to be exemplifying living meditation. The three power-tools that we discussed in this chapter—Keeping a Reminder, Selecting an Environment and Exercising Visualization—may prove effective to speed our progress. These tools, collectively or individually, are equally effective in meeting the purpose of any discipline, in any phase, of our lives.

- - - - - - - - - - -

Highlights of
The Living Meditation

(1) Add anything that you may have to in your daily life to encourage your visualization process, an act of "seeing" yourself having possessed already the qualities of poise and patience, the ones you are striving to enhance in your nature.

(2) Repeat your visualization process as often as you can, and hold its focus each day longer than before. Remember that what we think perpetually so we become eventually.

(3) Until meditation becomes a part of your daily life, anchor your mind to some sort of a reminder as my mother used a "knot" to her *sari* and my friend, a little statue of three monkeys in his key chain.

(4) Associate yourself with only those friends and environment, till your mind settles into your meditation that may encourage you to focus on the purpose of your discipline.

(5) Make efforts to admire those who possess such qualities, which you aspire to have in your own nature.

(6) The three tools: Keeping a Reminder, Selecting Environment and Exercising Visualization; each carries a power in its own way to influence you positively, but when used combined they bring the benefits faster and manifold regardless of the nature of the discipline you are working on. It could be of losing weight, earning more money, attaining a higher position, repairing a personal relationship or changing a habit.

= = = = = = = =

SECTION III
Meditation And Stress

Chapter 9
BENEFITS AT OUR HEALTH LEVEL

Chapter 10
BENEFITS AT OUR MENTAL LEVEL

Chapter 11
BENEFITS AT OUR EMOTIONAL LEVEL

Chapter 12
BENEFITS AT OUR SPIRITUAL LEVEL

MEDITATION AND STRESS

Introduction

My Approach

The subject of stress management may be discussed from different perspectives—medical, psychological, sociological, environmental, and philosophical. The approach of this book is certainly not medical; it is rather of a psychological, and more of a philosophical nature. It is psychological in a sense that meditation is primarily a mental discipline where the focus is to rise above the thought processes, and philosophical in a sense that the ultimate objective of meditation is self-transformation, to heighten our life's perception.

My whole focus is on how withdrawing ourselves daily for a few minutes, to relax and meditate, which may help us to better understand and manage the stress in our daily life. I have also experienced that this practice, irrespective of the name it is given, takes only a few minutes of our daily life but promises several benefits including reduced visits to physicians and medications. I have introduced here largely the same content that I have been practicing myself and presenting in my workshops, seminars and public lectures.

Those who had been practicing meditation and were influenced by its benefits in diverse areas of their lives such as health, temperament and relationships generously shared their experiences with me. Many of their personal testimonies, as well as of mine, have encouraged me to write the pages in this section, hoping that you too may feel encouraged to integrate this relaxation technique in your daily life and enjoy its benefits as others did.

It is our common experience that stress arises every time we are forced to adapt ourselves to a situation unfamiliar or uncomfortable to us. Let us examine few common scenarios in our daily life. An unexpected phone call from the workplace when we are vacationing, a key employee's inability to report to work on the very day when an important project is due, the automobile given for repairs is not ready at a promised hour or day, a long wait at a gas station or in a grocery store, backed up traffic, the young teenager is not back home at a reasonable time, flights delayed or cancelled are a few common stress-causing factors in our daily life. Do you, however, see something common among them? You are right, a feeling of "being caught unprepared" or a sense of utter helplessness.

We anticipate a situation to occur in a certain way or at a certain time, but it occurs differently. If we had foreknowledge of the phone call from the workplace, the late return of our teenager, or of the flight running late before our leaving home, the stress would be more manageable. The stress in these and similar illustrations is the result of a disparity between our expectation and reality. We shall discuss later how meditation may reconcile this gap.

Stress Is Not Always Negative

Stress can be positive too. A wedding or a child-birth in the family, an unexpected promotion or recognition at workplace, receiving a long coveted job offer, winning a jackpot, long desired overseas vacation, sudden meeting of a long lost friend, a new loving relationship, and a lucrative business deal are a few examples of positive stress.

These positive events equally cause us stress because they too at times come unexpected.

Nevertheless, they are welcome because they bring in our lives a sense of progress and happiness. These stresses are positive because they help us grow as an individual, a family, society or nation. Working hard to make more money for our children's higher education, and helping defend our country in a war are few more examples of inviting such stress in our lives.

Our life's basic urge for self-preservation would not be possible, nor would a civilization in any land be conceivable without bearing such stress. In a sense, stress regardless of its nature, positive or negative, is a situation that challenges one's psycho-physical make up, and demands a necessary alteration in one's lifestyle for survival and success. The focus of this writing is, what we identify as negative stress, which is a continual threat to our health, success and relationships, and to discuss how a regular practice of meditation may strengthen our overall natural immunity to diffuse its negative influence.

Two Characteristics of Stress

If you try to understand the following two characteristics of what is often experienced as stress, you will be in a better position to manage stress before it begins taking a toll on you.

(a) **Stress Is Subjective.** What is stressful to you may not be so stressful to me. Stress levels vary from person-to-person. Every human is different from others in his or her parental upbringing, educational background, influences of their peers and environment, and the nature of the past and prenatal experiences. All these factors form our overall attitude to the environment, society and life in general.

Allow me to illustrate my point through a common

scenario of our daily life. When caught in traffic, you may continue listening to the music or converse on your cellular phone showing little concern over the situation compared to the driver on your left demonstrating panic, or the driver on your right infuriated as though he is the victim of some secret plot. Every one of us responds differently to the same situation, which could be loss of work, illness in the family, tragedy in personal life or an impaired relationship.

Furthermore, things that are distressful for some may be pleasurable for others, for example, the riders on a steep roller coaster. There are some with their eyes shut, jaws clenched and holding the front bar with all their might. They can't wait to get out of this torture chamber. On the other hand, there are those who are with their eyes wide open, screaming and enjoying the thrill every moment of the ride.

How to take stress and reduce its negative effects largely depends on the angle of our life's perception and level of endurance. Those with a positive attitude are found to be, compared to others, more adaptable to changes and immune to the negative effects of the stress.

(b) Stress Is Time Sensitive. What is stressful to us now may not be so later. It varies in its intensity with time. How you suffered over the hostile behaviors of some of your peers during your high school years may not have the same impact on you today. This could be equally related to the situations in our lives such as of a crisis in our health, family finance, relationship or profession.

What seemed to be tormenting and unbearable at the time when we were passing through a certain period of our lives may not be so years later. There is also another side of this characteristic, and that is the change in our response. We react differently on the recurrence of the same situation. An occurrence matures us with a heightened sense of calmness and endurance to deal more firmly with the same event if it occurs again in our lives. A crisis makes us grow stronger and wiser when we refuse to flight, and are ready to face and learn.

All these examples conclude two points. **One, the same cause of stress generates different responses in different persons, and two, the same cause of stress may have different responses even in the same person at different times.** The following anecdote from the Buddha's life may best exemplify these two characteristics of stress.

The Buddha and Young Mother

A young mother's child died. The aggrieved mother, grasping the child in her arms, rushed to a physician. Placing the lifeless body before the physician, the mourning mother cried out for help. The physician, stunned and bewildered, guided the wailing mother to the Buddha who was visiting the town that day. The mother rushed again. Placing the child at the Buddha's feet, begging Him to bring her only child back to life. The Buddha consoled her to accept the inevitability of life. The Buddha's words fell on the wailing mother's deaf ears. Seeing the Buddha unresponsive, she declared that she would bring upon herself the same fate that her child suffered, if her wish was not granted.

The compassionate Buddha finally consented to show her mercy, if she met a small condition for Him. The Buddha finally declared: "Bring me a few mustard-seeds from that household in this village, which has never lost someone beloved to death." Leaving her child in the care of the Master and wiping her tears, the mother ecstatically set out in a hope, like a bullet. While pacing speedily the mother was calculating to herself joyfully that—The Buddha's condition was simple and His powers were great. I shall be seeing my child soon with his eyes open, and moving his tiny arms and legs.

Finally, the mother returned at the end of the day after a long wandering to where the Buddha was resting. She had discovered the answer of her enigma already. She was no longer screaming, crying and restless as before. She calmly threw herself at the feet of the Buddha in reverence, picked her child up and left in a stoical silence. She had realized the life's eternal truth. After knocking at the door of every house in the town, the mother had realized that death is an inseparable part of every life; it is inevitable and unpredictable.

What did you learn out of this story? It has helped me lately realize a two-fold message. One, the level of pain alleviates with time and growing receptive attitude. The mother's suffering did not remain anymore the same as it was before coming to the Buddha. Two, the level of perception is everything. After hearing the stories of death from all those householders whom she met, her point of view of life was transformed. The death of a dear one in the family, normally believed to be most stressful in our society at present, becomes less impacting with the dawn of a right perspective.

Have you read the book *Tuesdays With Morrie* by **Mitch Albom,** or seen the movie by the same name? The story embodies the same message that I wrote earlier. It is about the life's greatest lessons taking place between an old, wise man and a young, inquiring mind. **When we learn to accept our life in its totality, we suffer no longer the harmful effects of the stress.** Recognizing that the birth and death are the integral parts of our lives, leads our perception to a higher plateau.

The Hindus' law of Karma pronounces that we only have control over our actions and not always over their fruits, and whatever results come to us are at our own invitations by our acts or thoughts, directly or indirectly. When we accept this verdict we do not become vulnerable to the adverse effects of stress and the hostile behaviors of others as before anymore.

Life in the United States

The last World War has phenomenally changed our way of life. In just a few decades, our progress has touched the heights in many areas of our nation's growth, in science, agriculture, medicines, economics, transportation and space to name a few. This growth has enormously promoted our health and longevity, and materially improved our life style. Our single mindedness to pursuits and hard work led our nation to the highest peak of power and affluence making her worth emulating to other nations. All this, however, came at a high price to us. An urgency of times plagued our every activity in life including the family dinner, bedtime prayer, attending to our children and caring for our aged parents.

Someone observed that we have time to go to the moon, but no time to say 'hello' to our next-door neighbor; we have ears to hear the cry of a distant nation suffering a catastrophe, but not to hear the sigh of our dear ones in the nursing home. **George Carlin** put his observation in the following words:

> "We have multiplied our possessions but reduced our values. We talk of love but keep it limited to making love only. We visit church more but bring god in life less. We have learned how to make a living, but not a life. We have added years to our life but not life to our years."

Our concept of success has narrowed to the power of material possession and personal accomplishments. We restrict our pursuits to attaining the three Ps, Power, Position and Possession, and began measuring our success by those yardsticks. We personally grow more individualistic, and narrow our field of happiness to "me and mine." **This changed life style has brought us more material security, but it has deprived us of having a satisfying balance between our work and family, and a sense of personal contentment, the two major causes of increasing stress in our present lives.**

Knowing more about the strategy of our foes helps us to prepare ourselves better. Allow me to offer an analogy. While living in a crime afflicted vicinity we grow more alert in taking all possible measures to safeguard ourselves, our families and possession. We ensure before going to sleep and leaving home that all doors and windows are securely closed. We may have an extra latch installed on entrance doors for added security.

We may also have an electronic security system installed. We act more vigilantly on a suspicious movement in the neighborhood, train our children accordingly and may take a few personal safety lessons. In the same token, we need to study the nature of our foe; its nature of threats and impacts on varied realms of our lives and prepare ourselves with a lasting defense strategy.

A polluted environment, noise in streets, crowded trains and airplanes, traffic, inclement weather etc., though are common culprits of our daily stressful life, their impact on us is only to an extent that our level of immunity allows it. Rather than blaming the factors over which we possess little or no control, our prudence lies in discovering more ways to fortify our psychophysical system. This present Section of this book focuses on how meditation may accomplish this goal.

The remainder of the book endeavors to enhance two main points. One, examine the stress, its cause and effects. Rather than living mechanically and suffering helplessly under the dictates of the stress, investigate into its origin, examine its impacts and modify your life style if needed. Refuse to accept the stress as a myth or mandate of the environment we live in. The young mother in our illustration could reconcile with herself only after she discovered the truth of human life.

Two, focus on naturally developing your overall immunity. This could be attained at its best through nurturing the needs of all your faculties individually— the physical, psychological, emotional and spiritual.

I have dedicated each chapter of this section to the discussion of how a regular practice of meditation may help us build the natural immunity of each of our aforesaid faculties, finally developing within us an inner harmony, a power beyond all external powers combined, against the negative influences of the stress and threats of life.

= = = = = = = = = =

BENEFITS AT OUR HEALTH LEVEL

("Sit quietly, doing nothing, spring comes,
and the grass grows by itself."
Zen Koan)

Meditation, regardless of its focus, when practiced under the guidance of an experienced instructor, invariably improves one's pattern of breathing to be more rhythmic and diaphragmatic. This is a profound benefit of any relaxation technique like meditation. That is why I have highly recommended, in all the four methods discussed in the earlier Section, to focus on and count your breaths prior to the beginning of your meditation.

Regulated breathing helps calm our thoughts easier and relax our mind faster. It makes our breathing deeper, slower and infrequent. The main benefits of regulated breathing are more oxygen to our body, expansion of the lungs, and less stress on our heart to pump blood. However, when the very focus of our meditation is our breathing, it brings many benefits to our health and beyond. Let us now see how meditation benefits our overall health.

Major Benefits

(1) A uniform pattern of breathing supplies more

oxygen to our physiological system. The deeper the inhalation, the greater the amount of oxygen inhaled, improving our blood quality directly. Through the absorption of the purified blood, every cell and organ of our system grows healthier and more rejuvenated. The oxygenated blood brings added life to our overall health and years to our longevity.

(2) A good breathing exercise goes far beyond influencing the functions of the body's respiratory system and the organs connected to it. Our physiology is one whole unit. The revitalized functioning in one area equally impacts the functioning of other areas in our body. An improved respiratory system also enhances the effectiveness of other physiological processes such as of circulation, elimination, assimilation, metabolism and reproduction. Thus the functioning of our overall health is influenced positively.

(3) Deep, uniform breathing increases the level of endorphins, a natural painkilling chemical that our body naturally produces. This chemical possesses the power to boost our body's natural immunity, which makes us more immune to the normal aches and pains of our body. This is an important benefit of meditation to both our health and mind.

(4) Reduction in the breathing rate to as low as 12 from an average of 18 per minute in a regularly meditating healthy adult is another profound benefit. This takes some stress off our relentlessly operating heart. Even a small reduction in the operation of our heart produces a perceptible change in the health and life to this often overworked vital organ.

(5) According to a research on practitioners of the Transcendental Meditation, breathing under a deeply relaxed mind increases the frequency of the alpha waves in our brain from 10 to 12 cycles per minute.

This clearly suggests a heightened sense of our mental awareness although our eyes are closed and mind is quiet. A pattern of breathing and level of mental relaxation influence each other and impact the quality of our health accordingly.

(6) We have seen that the state of our mind is a determining factor of the state of our health. As we think, so do we enjoy or suffer our health. The state of our brain cells correspondingly influences our body cells. Our relaxed state of mind in meditation calms our body, its tensed organs, and physiological processes. A relaxed state of mind brings such a quality level of rest to our body that is not generally experienced even in our sleep. Though the body seems to be resting in our sleep, it is often disturbed by our mind's activities in its subconscious state such as dreams and nightmares.

Summary

Major benefits of meditation on health come from two areas. One is our relaxed mind, and second, our changed breathing pattern. Irrespective of the method practiced, meditation invariably improves our health, and adds years to our life. However, when meditation is practiced in conjunction with the suggested Warm-Up exercise in Chapter Three, it doubles the benefits in the realm of our health. A sincere and right practice promises a sound health and slowing of the aging process. The healthier we are, the more soundly we can withstand the adverse effects of the rising stress in our lives.

- - - - - - - - - -

Highlights of
Benefits At Our Health Level

(1) Focusing on your breaths during meditation naturally changes its pattern to more rhythmic and diaphragmatic.

(2) Breathing with awareness deepens our way of breathing, reduces its frequency and alleviates exertion off our incessantly beating heart. This promotes a better quality to the health and life of all our physiological organs, eventually increasing our longevity.

(3) Meditation, through its improved breathing pattern and increasingly relaxed mind profoundly influence our overall quality of health.

= = = = = =

10

BENEFITS AT OUR MENTAL LEVEL

"The mind . . . in itself can make
a heaven of hell and hell of heaven."
(John Milton)

Meditation is more a psychological discipline than merely the way of sitting, and counting of breathing. It is training our mind, helping change its focus and perception. Therefore, practicing meditation brings the most benefits to our psychological realm compared to any other realm of our lives.

(A) *High Level of Anxiety Reduced*

It is of common knowledge that the state of our mind correspondingly impacts our health, its physical counterpart. Our changing thoughts, moods and attitude constantly influence our physical cells. When we have good days in life or are mentally happy we enjoy good health. A stressful mind causes a stress in the body. A negative state of mind exhausts our physical vitality. Research shows that 72 % of our physiological complaints are mind related. Studies corroborate that 60 % of our visits to physicians are due to stress-related illnesses, with a state of anxiety predominant in it.

A chronic state of anxiety stands at the top among the factors responsible for our mental restlessness and disorders. Anxiety causes high blood circulation making our hearts overwork and tense our body. It is a major cause of our nervousness and perpetual stressful living. An anxiety-stricken attitude weakens our mind's functions, obscures our thinking and degenerates our health faster.

Nervousness, an advanced state of anxiety, is the over stimulation of the nerves, which keeps our consciousness confined to its physical level. Contrarily, a state of calmness promotes good health and the ability to make judgments better. Every stroke of anxiety imbalances some 27,000 billion cells in our body. Let's see how meditation may help an anxiety-stricken mind. It helps shift our mind's focus from its relentless thought processes to a state of relaxation. It helps transcend our thoughts voluntarily. Relaxing the mind for a little while is only the beginning of meditation. As the practice lasts longer and the level of concentration deepens with time, the mind's relaxed state extends to our behaviors while facing the challenges of our day-to-day life during our rest of the day.

With the growing sincerity in our meditation, the state of our mental calmness integrates into the very fabric of our nature. It may take time to reach this state, but it is not impossible. A relaxation technique like meditation is the only way that I know of that brings this desired result.

With the mind steadily growing calmer, the instances of high anxiety in our lives naturally diminish. This altered state of our nature positively influences other areas in our lives too, such as our health and relationships.

Beyond calming our anxiety-ridden mind, meditation goes one step further, working at its very root. Anxiety results from the fear of the unknown and a sense of insecurity in ourselves. Those who possess such a fear and lack a sense of self-confidence often suffer anxiety attacks, jeopardizing their own health eventually. Meditation helps alleviate the very cause of the undue anxieties through altering our belief system to a nature of "I have done my best, come what may, I shall happily face it." I have discussed more about this later in the chapter on the benefits of meditation at our spiritual level.

(B) Unhealthy Habits Changed

Generally, all habits find their ways in our lives in two kinds of circumstances. One, while trying out something the first time out of a sheer curiosity or the so-called innocent temptation, and then on liking it, we gradually get hooked to it. This is how the young adults in their adolescent years, often fall preys to unhealthy habits.

Two, when we experience something profoundly missing. It could be our self-esteem, personal security, work-satisfaction, success in life, failures in meeting ambitions, peace in our families, or a good companion to talk to. Those who have reached the height of success in their lives are often found addicted more than others. Contrarily, those who are religious minded, having a strong sense of reaching out to others, surrounded by trusting friends or having a strong family support are seldom prey to bad habits.

An inclination to trying out a new thing is generally a result of something that we have inherited from our parents, or that we have brought with us from our previous lives as the theory of reincarnation in certain faiths pronounces. When I tried to offer my daughters when they were of some ten years of age, a lighted cigarette to puff or an alcoholic drink to sip they never felt an urge for it, opposed to a natural attraction to experiment of inquisitive minds at this age in a friendly environment.

When the first time experiment becomes a part of our way of living, it is difficult, if not impossible, to change. In such an instance, meditation helps us to change our habit by raising our sense of awareness and making us realize that the habit impedes our spiritual journey.

A habit in the second kind of people is a means to temporarily forget the painful occasions such as of failures and rejections of the past, and loneliness in the present. A bad habit fills the subtly tormenting gap often generated between what we possess and what we don't, what we are and what we wish to be. These minds suffer another illness, the illness of self-created complex of inferiority resulted from competitive comparison with others. I picked up a habit of smoking at my early age due to this reason. I was trying to show off to senior peers that I was already mature to their level, and that I was more than what I seemed.

Forming an unhealthy habit is our mind's ingenious way to express its state of dissatisfaction with its present state, and divert its attention to something that seems to be providing solace and happiness. **Habits make their ways into our lives subtly and gradually. We invite them in our lives as our friends, only to regret later.**

I have shared, in the previous Section, how I once overcame my sweet tooth at one stage in my life when the work was insipid and the hours were long. It was the way of my clever mind to forget what it did not like to think. The sense of awareness heightened through the regular practice of meditation rendered me a different perception and necessary strength in my resolve to change myself.

A right practice of meditation never allows an unhealthy habit to form in the first place. An unhealthy habit is the one that impedes our true progress and well-being, the one that obscures our clear thinking and vision of our future. With time, maturity of meditative practice dissolves the sense of insecurity dominating our attitude. We begin experiencing a sense of contentment at our best in every situation. We grow more adaptable and tolerant to adversities in our lives.

We realize the worthlessness of material comparativeness with others, generally a major cause of our mental restlessness. We no longer experience the gap, often painful, between what we are and what we wish to be. We seldom find those who are into a discipline of self-exploration like meditation ever subjected to an unhealthy habit, or a complex of inferiority or superiority.

(C) Overcoming Others' Negative Attitudes

According to an Arabic saying, a family is a human-made paradise on earth. It should offer peace and comfort when a husband, wife, or child returns home after their long day's battle. Nevertheless, it often fails to meet these promises founded on. The incidents of conflicts over trivial affairs and, at times, mistrust makes the life in the family stifling and unbearable. The stressful environment, whether at work or home, poses the situation of fight or flight. Ironically, neither seems practical to a right minded person. It appears, at times, that our life's candle is burning at both ends making our life burdensome, and eventually causing our health to suffer. Have you ever passed through such a period in your life? Generally, the answer is yes. I think that we all face such situations, at one time or another, in our lives when no third alternative seems practical.

Wise people advise however of a third alternative: of developing a sense of personal indifference, a sense of indifference to what is detrimental to our growth. They advise us to be like a lotus flower. The lotus grows and spends all its life in the water, and yet it remains unattached to the water. They advise us to interact with our transitory world like the lotus with the water. Do you remember an illustrative **Chinese statue of three little monkeys** sitting side-by-side, conveying a timeless message on how to live in the world made of all opposites such as good and bad alike? One monkey is seen covering his mouth with his hands, the second, his ears, and the third, his eyes.

Each of these monkeys offers a profound message how to live successfully without ever losing our self-composure—acknowledge both the good and the evil coexisting around you, and yet, learn to mentally tuning out what is not worthwhile to your progress. **How to develop such perception of tuning to what is worthwhile and tuning out to what is worthless to our growth is not shown in the conventional classrooms of schools and universities, nor in the training programs and workshops at workplaces.** We are therefore left to discover the ways to develop such a sense of perception by ourselves.

One effective way to develop such a state of perception is to turn within us with a receptive mind. This is the way of Meditation. It helps transform our perception and ingrain it into our nature. It works this way. During the early period of practicing meditation, our untrained mind naturally combats with the distracting factors of both the restless mind within and the noise outside, for example, children playing, cars passing, neighbors talking, lawn mowing, or the telephone ringing. One's struggle to overcome the influences of these distracting factors is a common experience of all those who are new to this discipline.

Nevertheless, this struggle is only in the beginning.

Paramahansa Yogananda gives an illustration of muddy water in a glass. When a glass just filled with soiled water and placed on an even surface, we observe the particles slowly settling at the bottom, leaving the water at the top clearer and calmer'than before. In the same way, when we begin meditating with a resolve to relax, our thoughts begin gradually settling down, enabling us to rise above the distracting influence of our thoughts.

As our practice deepens with time, our field of awareness expands. We grow oblivious to the thoughts and the outside uproars. This is called the sense of personal indifference. The noises may still be there in our surroundings, but they do not distract us now as they did before.

Our altered perception in meditation could be equally applied to our real life situations. We are in a position now to demonstrate the changed state of attitude, the attitude of personal indifference to the hostile words and behaviors of others at work or in relationships. We are able to act dispassionately to what is not useful to our lasting interest. We are now no more personally sensitive as before to the supervisor's disdainful remarks, coworker's spiteful talks or spouse's unfriendly comments.

We are now able to draw a line between what is and what is not healthy for us, what to accept and what to ignore. We develop a discriminatory sense like that of the royal swan in Hindu mythology. When offered a bowl of milk mixed with water the swan is said to be drinking the milk only and leaving the water behind.

Similar is an attitude exemplified by ants, if you have ever carefully observed. The behavior of an ant, walking on your kitchen counter scattered with few mixed grains of sugar and salt, might amaze you. You would find the ant circling around the grain of sugar and trying to drag it to some safe place. It will not bother itself to take even a second look at the grain of salt. Even an ant has a natural 'insight' to distinguish between what to accept and what to discard. This is what meditation does to us, developing a sense of insight and personal indifference like the Swan and the ant.

This transformed attitude makes us more invulnerable to the negative and provocative situation, and keeps us more focused only on what is conducive to our personal growth. In a sense, we grow self-oriented from the state of the 'other-oriented'. (Know that I am speaking of 'self-oriented', not 'self-centered'.) Our impulsive behavior now transforms into the self-composed one toward the unpleasant encounters at work, on the road, and in our families. Though still dealing with the same people and situations, they no longer dictate us as before. Now, we enjoy more power with endured poise and mental equanimity.

(D) Self-Esteem Enhanced

A tendency of thinking of ourselves as inferior originates from two sources: One, inherited attitudes from parents, and two, attitudes developed along the way of our growth wherein the childhood experiences are greatly responsible. A habit of comparing ourselves with others is often a cause of our low self-esteem. Allow me to ask you, "Have you ever returned home from a social gathering with a sense of lowness about yourself?" If I have to respond to this question, my honest answer would be, "Yes, I have on numerous occasions." Many of you may relate to what I am about to share with you.

I used to return from socials with a sense of inferiority. Finding others with worldly powers more than what I possessed would make me feel inferior in their presence. This could be related to anything, their physical stature, personality, position at work, social status, material affluence, sophisticated language, scholastic achievement or public recognition. With this experience, though acting normal outwardly, I would not be the same inwardly on my way back home. Do you relate to such an experience in your life?

Why do such feelings of lowness ever overshadow our joy, and at times, chase us? We were rather looking forward to attending such an event probably days before, and lo behold, we leave the event rather dispirited. On retrospection, we observe that no one had hurt us, offended or demeaned us, and yet, we left the event in disappointment. According to my observation, all ambitious minds suffer this experience on varied levels. Have you ever examined: "Where does such feeling of self-hurt come from? What did actually happen between you and those whom you met?"

Allowing this feeling to find a niche in our consciousness is dangerous to us later in our lives. It may cause a major mental disorder to the extent of depression. We should therefore be discreet when comparing ourselves with others. **A comparison that inhibits our growth is not healthy for us.** We should rather train our mind to focus on those qualities in others, which may encourage us to succeed and excel further. Remember that what we perpetually think, so do we eventually become. **Ralph Waldo Emerson** wrote, "Be very careful with what you set your heart upon, for you will surely have it."

An ideal attitude for me is to rise above all comparisons with others. Those who are subjected to a complex of superiority are no better than their counterparts either; they too suffer an inner imbalance. Inferiority and superiority, both have the same origin except that each expresses itself differently. **An Eastern saying** goes, "For one to belittle others, the one has to be little first."

Another source of our low self-esteem is our mental tendency to dwell on the regrets and failures of our past. We do not realize that the time gone never returns and that the key to peace in our lives lies in accepting and compromising with what is beyond our control. Such realization requires us to change ourselves from inside. **That is why the conventional training programs on developing self-esteem and assertiveness often fail in producing long-term effects.** How can an external treatment work effectively on an internal ailment? Practicing meditation is one such way that I have personally experienced as effective in helping us alter from within.

Meditation helps us in two ways: One, changing our mental attitude of comparing ourselves with others negatively, and two, compromising with our past. Meditation is a way to look within and know more about ourselves. It is a way of self-communion and self-acceptance. We accept ourselves as one whole entity, endowed with perfection and imperfection, good and bad, strength and weaknesses alike.

We must learn to accept our past, no matter how unpleasant, to fully enjoy the achievements of our present and dream of our future. This state of total acceptance of ourselves forces the door open naturally for our self-improvement in place of the thoughts of self-denial and self- condemnation.

The sense of self-acceptance brings self-compromise where all people and events of the past, pleasant and unpleasant alike, are viewed as visitors crossing our path with the only purpose to enhance our own growth. The more we are integrated within, the sounder we are in a position to manage what is imperfect to others in our lives. Our transformed mental and emotional energies now focus more on our present, making our future more rewarding and enjoyable.

Summary

We discussed how meditation positively works on hypertension, mental nervousness, low self-esteem, unhealthy habits and negative attitudes displayed to us by others. It works not only in curing these problems; it works at their very root. While discussing about developing a sense of personal indifference, an attitude of not identifying yourself with other's hostile behavior, I offered you the examples of the statuette of three monkeys, royal swan, ants and lotus in the water. This attitude is the only key to achieve the most in our lives, known to all observing minds and yet, ironically, cannot be taught in the conventional classrooms and training programs.

- - - - - - - - - -

Highlights of
Benefits At Our Mental Level

(1) When the level of calmness attained during your meditation grows longer and pervades your interactions with the world, your levels of anxiety and hypertension naturally reduce.

(2) States of perpetual anxiety, hypertension and low self-esteem result often from a sense of insecurity in ourselves. You will seldom find meditative minded persons ever exhibiting such negative characteristics.

(3) Often, the sense of low self-esteem and unhealthy habits make their ways in our lives when we suffer a state of loneliness. The more you engage yourself into some mental relaxation discipline like meditation where you feel self-expanded, or some creative pursuits where you feel most self-expressive, the more you will enjoy the state of self-fulfillment, a state opposed to the state of loneliness.

(4) Habits make their way in our lives as our long sought dear friends, but when our philosophical reorientation awakens in the recesses of our meditative silence, we soon discover how wrong we were in our judgments.

(5) The more you avoid being caught into competitive comparison with others, the faster you will regain your natural self-esteem. The silent self-commune in your meditation will help you attain it.

(6) Self-acceptance is a key to making the best of your present and molding your future. When self-divided within, your efforts to build your future is like building a castle on the sand.

= = = = = = = = = =

BENEFITS AT
OUR EMOTIONAL LEVEL

*"Meditation is an effort in the beginning.
Later on it becomes habitual and gives bliss, joy and peace."*
(Swami Sivananda)

We have discussed the benefits of meditation at our physical level and mental level respectively in the last two chapters. Now, we undertake the discussion of benefits of meditation at our emotional level.

You might have observed that some people appear temperamentally impulsive in their behaviors. They act rather quickly and cannot wait till others finish their point of view. Their attitude is often dictated by their emotions compared to their reasoning.

We all at times behave this way in some degree, but the predominance of emotions, especially the negative ones, in temperament is harmful to us, and more so when expressed publicly. Little do such temperamental people realize that their own nature is responsible for troubles in their lives. Unrestrained anger, deep-rooted jealousy, a strong tendency of personal likes and dislikes, and faltering moods are the examples of such negative emotions. We shall refer to them as unhealthy emotions.

In a sense, every emotion regardless of its nature,

is positive. Emotions become negative and undesirable only when they are expressed unduly and inappropriately. A mother's chastisement to her child is perfectly fine, but when done out of her unmanaged anger or making it a public spectacle is inappropriate. Those with unmanageable emotions are restless inwardly as much as outwardly. Though helpful and good hearted, they behave often unpredictably. They invite troubles in their lives such as endangering jobs, fracturing relationships, distancing themselves from coworkers, jeopardizing professional success and risking their health.

One may wonder as to where such unhealthy emotions in life originate from. High blood pressure, heredity and inadequate parental training during their pre-adolescent years seem to be the culprit factors. The sooner we detect these traits in our nature and identify their origins, the faster we can take charge of them, preventing further damage in our relationships with the world. I can relate to these emotions because I was once a victim of one of them myself. My unhealthy emotion was eruptive anger.

When these emotions are left unchecked, like the randomly fired bullets, they only devastate our relationships at work or in family. Contrarily, when they are suppressed, they create mental disorders. Therefore, we must find a third way beyond their erratic expression and repression. We must learn to regulate this energy. **No energy, positive or negative, ever dies; it simply changes its form.**

Negative energy when harnessed and directed in a positive direction doubles our progress. It is like the force of water which may otherwise destroy the fields and villages, but when regulated could be transmuted into electricity or hydraulic energy, a dynamic positive force improving the lives of many.

Meditation promises this alchemy.

Meditation helps transform energy of negative emotions into positive strength in two ways: Witnessing and Visualization.

(A) The Technique of Witnessing

A regular practice of withdrawing ourselves from all thoughts and emotions, starting with few minutes daily, enables us to rise above emotions and train our mind to view them dispassionately. During the first few minutes of meditation, we may experience our mind cluttered with thoughts and the related emotions. It may seem to be a frightening experience, if you are a beginner. You may think that you would never be able to penetrate the chaotic state, and attain the restful state promised by the books and teachers.

Our primary obstacle in meditation, regardless of the nature of practice followed, is the distractions of noise and thoughts. The captured sensation by our mind of the outside noise adds to our already existing restless state of mind, making it more difficult to focus. These thoughts when fed by their corresponding emotions become doubly difficult to manage, especially by the beginners.

However, I may say based on my personal experiences that if you hold your patience and continue to meditate, you will surely reach the state of separating your thoughts from their emotions as I could. Watching your emotions from a distance, even only momentarily, in the beginning, is still a clear sign of your progress in the right direction.

Simply witnessing and not getting carried away by those negative emotions such as greed, anger, and impulsive temperaments, which might have long dominated our minds, is certainly a difficult discipline for an untrained mind, but not impossible. The state of relaxation where all our thoughts and emotions are fully merged and rested, though just for a little while in the beginning, can be endured longer with time, helping us gain more power over our emotions. Months later, you will be able to experience the desired change in your behavior effortlessly. The longer is the period of successful witnessing in meditation, the greater is the influence of that mental state in our interactions with others during the rest of the day.

(B) The Technique of Visualization

The other way meditation helps harness our hardened emotions is through the technique of visualization. It is a psychological technique to recondition the grooves of our mind making them such that they become more conducive to what our mind desires to be. It is a way to mentally imagine that we have already realized the state that we are still striving to attain, and hold that image under our mental focus for as long as possible. I have discussed this technique in several places earlier in this book, particularly in Chapter Two.

Perhaps, a struggle in my personal life may better illustrate how this technique could be effectively exercised. When seized by anger at one stage in my life, my behavior in those years was erratic and often unpredictable. I lacked a sense of tolerance and concentration, the two cardinal virtues for healthy relationship with others and personal success. When trifling issues would cause my anger to erupt, it would instantly get out of my control, making me often feel sorry for myself later.

I could arrest its progression by altering my meditative practice. This altered practice was a blend of three methods of meditation on breathing, affirmation, and especially visualization. In this practice, I focused on my breaths, and used to visualize that the positive energy of peace was flowing in while inhaling, and that the negative energy of anger was flowing out while exhaling.

In other words, every cell of my body and mind was imbibing peace, drop by drop, with fresh air through my every inhalation, and similarly, every cell was flushing out anger, drop by drop, with discarded air through exhalation. I have discussed this personal anecdote of my struggle and success, elsewhere in this book with further details.

I may admit today that I am not completely free of anger, but the anger does not catch me off guard as it did before. I foresee it gradually building up; this gives me time to prepare myself. I move away for a few minutes from the spot, or try to mentally withdraw myself, shifting my mind off the cause of restlessness. I re-stated this experience from my personal life in this chapter only to show you that a right method of meditation possesses power to change our unhealthy emotions no matter how unhealthy and chronic.

My experience on several occasions have validated that once we are serious with a discipline of self-improvement, further guidance and support, encouraging us on our journey, come to us mysteriously when needed. The sooner the causes of unhealthy emotions, which draw subtly and relentlessly on our positive energy, are detected, the quicker we shall be able to free ourselves from the instances of embarrassments, regrets and sufferings in our personal lives.

Overwhelming emotions when demonstrated

frequently, obscures our thinking and compels us to behave insanely. **Emotional imbalance generates stress.** The more we demonstrate self-composure in expressing our emotions, the more we can prevent the instances of discords and disharmonies in our relationships with others, often a major cause of our stressful living.

Summary

Negative emotions are the ones that obscure our discriminatory sense of distinguishing right from wrong, and obstruct our true progress. In a sense, every emotion, irrespective of its nature, when expressed unchecked and inappropriately, is unhealthy. No matter how unhealthy the emotion, it is not prudent to suppress or release it unchecked. A modified meditative practice shows a third alternative, healthier and more practical to suppression or uncontrolled release. When the power of a negative emotion transforms into a positive one, our positive energy compounds, instances of stress reduce and the speed of our progress doubles.

- - - - - - - - - -

Highlights of
Benefits At Our Emotional Level

(1) Emotions, positive or negative, which have a tendency to erupt and grow unmanageable, take a high toll on all phases of our lives, success, health and mainly on relationships. We must work on them.

(2) Meditative introspection, a process of knowing ourselves at a deeper level, is a more effective tool than the doctors' offices and therapies, to identify the origins of our unhealthy emotions.

(3) Meditative awareness behind our closed eyes possesses a power, greater than our medical prescriptions, to manage our emotions. I have explained how it rescued me once to overcome the dictates of anger in my personal life.

(4) A meditative discipline, when combined with the techniques of *witnessing*, visualization and affirmation, gains an added force to transform the negative energies of emotions, and speed our progress in all realms of our lives.

(5) No emotion, positive or negative, ever dies; it only changes its form, for example, the floodwaters converted into hydraulic energy. No energy is negative as such; it depends on how we outlet it. Even a positive emotion embarrasses and hurts us if released unchecked. Meditation awakens our intuitive faculty, helping us discriminate between the positive and negative.

= = = = = = = = =

BENEFITS AT
OUR SPIRITUAL LEVEL

"What lies behind us and what lies before us
are tiny matters compared to what lies within us."
(Ralph Waldo Emerson)

Having discussed in previous chapters the benefits of meditation in our physical, mental and emotional levels of our lives, we discuss now, in this final chapter of the book, the benefits of meditation in our spiritual realm. I occasionally compare human life with a square with the sidelines representing our emotional and mental faculties, and the top line with the physical one. The whole square stands on our spiritual faculty, the base line.

The more the base is sound, the more the square of our life is sound. The spiritual faculty is the most important among all our faculties and forms a central cord to our existence. The more this faculty is nurtured, the stronger is our life within as well as without, making stronger our overall immunity naturally. Those who realize this are found to be more collected and happier than others.

After all, it is our perception of life and its place in the world that determines our level of happiness. It is our concept of success that determines the level of our success. Our belief system is everything, more than the sum total of all our material possessions and achievements.

Spirituality to me is not a talk of personal gods and faiths, of heaven and hell. I rather talk of awakening our conscience, finding the meaning of rituals and recognizing our philosophical perception that helps us distinguish between right and wrong. I refer to our sense of wisdom that reminds us time after time to stay in the center amidst our daily priorities. Aristotle called it the golden path, and the Buddha called it the middle path. My reference is to our conscience, above our mind's eternal thought processes. Regardless of one's faith, one will not deny the fact of having a conscience or a sense of wisdom.

We have discussed the benefits of meditation in our physical, mental and emotional faculties in the preceding chapters. Now, let us see how meditation benefits our spiritual faculty, with a focus on better managing the rising stress and its adverse effects in our lives.

I have discussed the following five major benefits:

(1)   A Loyal Companion Discovered
(2)   Middle-Age Crisis
(3)   Seeking Perfection Is Not Always A Virtue
(4)   "What's not yours let it go"
(5)   Spiritual Evolution: Our Soul's Ultimate Quest.

(1)   A Loyal Companion Discovered

A renowned thinker once said that if all human wants and needs are narrowed down to two basic necessities, those would be: **Finding a purpose to welcome tomorrow, and a loyal companion to talk to.**

I wish to focus here on our basic mental craving for having someone to talk to, someone to share with, someone to seek for counsel when in difficulty and solace when dejected.

Do you ever experience loneliness or missing someone in your life someone who genuinely cares to understand and listen to you? If your answer is yes, know that you are not alone. You might have wondered at times that despite having so many people around you, spouse, children, cousins, friends, parents and peers in your life, why there seems to be no one close enough to turn to.

I believe that most human relationships emerge out of our personal needs, physical, mental or emotional. Though married and living together for several years, husband and wife may not be finding themselves in harmony with each other all the time. In such cases, a true sense of belonging between the two is found missing. A long stay together of two individuals, even in close relationship, does not necessarily promise a level of intimacy. A bond between the two, particularly in a husband-wife relationship, comes only when the relationship rises above their level of physical consciousness. With time, the relationship should rise to the soul-level, beyond the emotional and mental levels. Such a relationship is sometimes found with other than one's spouse; it could be with a sibling or friend.

Not until we have someone close whom we can fully trust, we continue experiencing deep within us a sense of loneliness and helplessness. Such a relationship is beyond all expectations and conditions; so simple and yet, nearly impossible to find in life. Allow me to offer a couple of illustrations.

Be This Not Your Life!

When diagnosed with a cancer of pancreas, a mother of three and grandmother of two was shocked and in sheer tears. Instead of breaking the news to her husband and seeking his comfort, she felt withdrawn from him. She knew how her husband would react to the news. She feared that she would have to hear unpleasant words in place of few consoling words that she most needed at this hour.

What a stressful period of life for a husband and wife living under the same roof and sharing the same bed, and yet due to some personal differences, more often than not trifling, keeping them far apart! After the children are grown and settled, husband and wife should strive to come closer through more opening to and better knowing about each other. She knew how her husband would react to the news. Rather than few words of comfort and support, he would bluntly point out to her how negligent she has been in keeping up with her health.

He would say, "Didn't I caution you to be more careful with your health? Didn't I ask you to go for medical check up regularly? Didn't I remind you to watch your weight and diet? And so on." She bore the agony of her predicament to herself for days before she could disclose her condition to her husband. **Compared to the actual pain, the very thoughts of the pain causes more pain, and even more unbearable yet, is the situation of not having someone to openly talk to.** This is what I mean by a time of loneliness in life. Many in old age, when living alone due to marital separations or death of their spouses, are found to be suffering from a severe loneliness-syndrome.

Another such example is from the life of Cheryl. She seemed to be in her early thirties and having a successful professional career. In one of my seminars, Cheryl shared with me a painful period of her life that she was then passing through in the somewhat following words. When in her apartment by herself, she felt quite insecure. When alone, a strong wave of sadness would seize her. Often, she felt like crying out loudly when she was alone in her apartment, for no apparent reason.

She had no clue of what was happening to her or why. This change in her behavior had only surfaced recently. If it had to do with the unpleasant memories of her past, she did not know what was triggering them. She obviously needed a wise and trusting friend during those hours that would act as her catalytic agent, encouraging her to open up and unburden herself. The period of being alone was so painful to her that she would hesitate to return to her apartment until making sure that one of her roommates was there.

Cheryl represents most of us at some point of time in our lives. What further adds to this situation of pains and stress caused by such loneliness-syndrome is that the health care practioners, on whom we depend for cure, cannot be of much help in such scenarios as well. They cannot diagnose the causes of the ailments of the patients like Cheryl. Let us see how a practice of meditation may help relieve us of such sense of emptiness in our lives.

Meditation helps us in two ways: One, getting used to liking ourselves, and two, occasional signs from within us suggesting a presence of some power higher than us.

While meditating we are all alone. It is a very difficult situation for us in the beginning to feel comfortable with the new discipline. **Often, our greatest fear is to be alone.** We fear ourselves, and feel secured in the presence of others, even if they are strangers. Our own past scares us. In a session of guided meditation, when I ask my students to close their eyes, I observe that it is very difficult for some. They will open their eyes and quickly look around to feel secured though they are with the like-minded peers and in a familiar surrounding. It is human nature.

It takes a sort of training and patience to stay inwardly active with our eyes closed. Once we get accustomed to meditation, we begin feeling comfortable with ourselves. We begin enjoying our own company and rise above the fear of loneliness more day by day. This is the profound benefit of regular meditation that nothing else in the world can match.

The other way meditation helps us alleviate our loneliness-syndrome is as follows. As I have suggested in the introduction of this Section, the only purpose of meditation in most major faiths in the East is finding God. I have conveniently avoided taking spirituality to this extent, and have made references of the conscience, sixth sense, higher power, etc., instead.

When the state of deep relaxation is realized in meditation, our consciousness transcends our physical consciousness and tunes with a higher or super consciousness. In this state, we are said to be experiencing the presence of an entity, a supernatural power that may have been heard or read of, but never personally encountered before.

The presence of this power is normally felt by way of occasionally witnessing the phenomena such as a light without source, candle light, falling star, descending dove, gentle music, and sound of a bell or chime. Most common among these is the hearing of an inner voice.

Such encounters are felt more clearly and frequently as our practice deepens with time. They are ever there in us, but not felt due to our mind's preoccupations with the worldly pursuits. It is like the distant mountains obscured by heavy fogs. As our mental tranquility deepens with increasing meditation, our psychic abilities begin unfolding before us making us "see" with our eyes closed, as it happened in the life of Helen Keller who was mute, deaf and blind, and yet could recognize people by her mere touch.

When the presence of some friendly entity is felt within, our dependence on others in the world reduces. We find someone within us ever present to comfort us in distress, to guide us in a difficulty, and listens when we are overwhelmed. When we encounter such an experience, we feel no longer helpless like the long married woman with a cancer, or lonely like Cheryl.

(2) Middle-Age Crisis

There comes a time, generally around middle age, which is an enormously stressful period in our lives for no apparent reason. This stress seems to arise from all corners of our lives, physical, mental, and spiritual, which if not dealt with calmly and prudently may devastate the rest of the years of our lives.

A realization of not having lived all our past years the way we wanted to, often troubles us, particularly when we are in our late forties. Around this point of time in our lives when we have almost settled in our work, family relationship, and other worldly pursuits, our mind tends to be more reflective and critical over our past decisions during the previous years. This is the threshold period of our lives separating our youth and the ensuing old age.

By this age, our professional schooling and training are over, our career is settled, children are grown and gone, and the planning for the retirement period is almost charted out. After the hustle and bustle of the youthful years, now is the time when we generally reflect over the bygone years and contemplate over the future as far we can see. We grow most concerned and anxious about our life at this point of our age.

Do you relate to what I mean? Well, you might wonder why all this mental restlessness seems to be upsurging right around this age in our lives? Why should such period in life arise at all, and if it had to come why not earlier when we were younger to face it better? Here is my explanation.

Our body reminds us of its aging process, and our mind of not having yet achieved enough. It is the very nature of our mind to achieve more regardless of the condition of its physical counterpart, our body. It continually oscillates between the regrets for not using wisely the opportunities in the past, at one end, and the anxieties of overall insecurities and uncertainties of our future, at the other end.

Perhaps, that is why this time of life is called the period of middle-age crisis, the period of self-reflection and inner tension, the period of self-dissatisfaction and of endeavoring harder to achieve more. If you have not experienced, around this age in your life the state of inner conflict that I am referring to here, it may either simply baffle you or you may not have observed it from this perspective. Allow me to present our mind's state around this time with some common examples.

This juncture in our lives reminds us of countless occasions when we might have exercised better judgments. The regrets come from different parts of our lives. The things that we did not do, the roles that we did not play well, the projects we never completed, the people and places we missed to visit, the promises we failed to meet, and the decisions we could not make timely. The career we could not choose, the training, discipline and support we could not render to our children, the high school sweetheart we could not marry, the level of care we failed to give to our parents, and so on and so forth.

Perhaps, that is why this period of our lives is called the period of crisis and reflection, the period of strife between a critical mind and its joy seeking heart. Perhaps, that is why those who are around this age are labeled "over the hill', and use black balloons to celebrate their birthdays.

For these several reasons, people with reflective and ambitious minds do not feel at peace with themselves around this period of their lives. Even those having financial securities enough for the rest of their lives seem to be restless within. It is strife between our mind and heart, one is seeking more to possess, and the other, seeking contentment in what it possesses. As we know that **inner disharmony supplies a breeding ground to stress.** An analogy from our daily life that comes to my mind may interest you. It is the hour at the end of the day when we still have a long way to go with our papers and meetings, and our body and mind are nearly exhausted of the long day's work.

Our Fight Must Continue

You may ask, "How can we reconcile the distance between our mind and heart? How can we compromise with our present?" My answer is simple and straight; first fight out the situation until you cannot fight anymore at all, before you even consider compromising with your present. Examine your mind's complaints objectively. If you think it is right, and you still have resources such as time, age, money and physical stamina, go all the way to accomplish it. There is no short cut.

Untimely compromising is make-believe to ourselves. The mind may be quiet for a while. It will arise again with more force to chase you. That situation may bring stress into your life more than you can bear. Whatever way you think you can meet your mind's legitimate complaints, I would say, go for it. Do not unduly procrastinate. You have to get over with it as long as you can. Do not try to quiet your mind with convenient excuses. It is simply a patch up with your present, failing to bring you a sense of lasting satisfaction.

You are never too late, especially in areas of learning for your personal growth and reaching out to others. One ex-colleague of mine had started learning Spanish at the age of 57 after she was retired from her job. Once I had a peer in his late sixties to learn Internet skills. You can still change your career, job or profession. You still can get back into the regime of a physical workout or join the workforce. You still can find a source for extra income and do more saving. You are never too late to catch up in relationships. All it takes is a slight shift in our attitude. Beside the change in pace, you can still do it.

Here is **a scenario from my personal life**. When I was attending the University of Bombay in my early 20s, I had developed an ambition then to lecture and teach adults like a professor in classrooms. In light of the fast changing circumstances after my graduation and marriage, it never seemed possible to have that ambition materialize. And, lo behold, some 30 years later today, what I am professionally doing is the same that I had aspired to do then. I started a new career against occasionally receiving discouraging words, and I never thought even once that it was too late. This was the only way, I thought, to transcend the likely stressful period in my life.

Nevertheless, we cannot do anything at anytime in our lives. We have to accept our limitations and learn to compromise with ourselves at a certain stage in life. After judging the state of your health, if you think you cannot do much about your mind's complaints and regrets, find the ways to compromise with your present, which is the only choice.

Compromising is not easy. In its eternal quest to rise and succeed more, it is absolutely contrary to the nature of our mind to compromise with itself. Therefore, **we need to go beyond our mind, because the very cause cannot cure itself.** Our mind knows only to analyze and investigate as opposed to synthesize and reconcile. We must rise above our mind to find ways and receive help. The faculty above our thinking one is our philosophical faculty.

Reaching our philosophical faculty means altering our life's perception, the perception of events and situations in our lives. Meditation promises this attainment. The very objective of meditative practice is to rise above our mind—its processes of thinking, judging and analyzing. This transforms our perception to our day-to-day battles of our past as well as of our present.

We cannot suppress our mind. In the light of our altered perception, our mind may develop an understanding: "I did my best that I could in the given situation at that time." "Among the conflicting priorities, I exercised the best possible judgment then."

"I have no control over the outcome. I know deep down however that I conducted myself most prudently that I could in the given circumstances."

With time, the gap between the regrets and complaints of the past at one end, and the worries and anxieties of the future at the other end, will naturally reconcile by itself, enabling you to live fully into the very moment of your present. This is the only way how we can turn normally the stressful period of our lives into an enjoyable one. This is how my practice of meditation has benefited me.

(3)   Seeking Perfection Is Not Always A Virtue

I wish to discuss here the benefits of meditation in the lives of those who seek perfection in themselves as well as in others around them. I have observed that such a tendency of mind generates friction with others, paralyzes relationships and causes stress in own lives. It often proves to be a self-invited curse to us rather than a virtue.

Have you ever come across such people: Who seek everything in as well as around them impeccable? Who see faults in all but themselves? Who think of themselves better than others? If you have observed them closely, you might have found one characteristic common in them. They are not happy with themselves. Their mind is often tense and agitated. They may be good-hearted, high achievers and living testimonies of some noble values, but they are not at peace with themselves. Their whole attitude is 'other-oriented'. Their expectations from others are unreasonably high.

A few more examples from the behaviors of these people may help you to identify them better. They expect their meetings to start and end at the precise time, the traffic on the road to move on, the waiter in a restaurant waiting on them only, their flights to take off and land at the scheduled time, or the physician and his staff available at an appointed hour. They get restless at a slightest change in their planned schedule of the day. A small change in predicted weather and a planned schedule would tick their moods off. I knew a young businessman who would turn angry on his wife on seeing the food at the dinner different than what they had agreed to previous night.

Little do these people realize that **seeking perfection in an imperfect world is like chasing a rainbow which is simply impractical.** They lose their sleep over the loss of a dime instead of rejoicing over the dollar found. They are overly particular about every small detail in their lives; their appearances, attires, shoes, cars, books, etc. The slightest variation or disorder in the arrangement of their things may upset them for hours. What would you advise these people so that they could be happier, get along with others better, and enjoy their lives a little more? I have presented below my answer through the case of Chris, who often behaved as a perfectionist.

Do You Relate To Chris?

For our convenience, let us name him Chris. He seemed to be obsessed with having his desk in the morning exactly the way he had left it the previous evening. Finding even one thing on his desk moved from its original position would upset him the next morning. Having discovered a disruption of his desk's arrangement, the normally jovial and easygoing Chris would not exchange a word with anyone for a couple of hours.

He admitted that he behaved the same way in his home, which often resulted in unwarranted arguments with his wife. People with such an attitude make others' lives around them equally miserable, often unknowingly. Their level of anxiety is high and endurance is low. They hurt and get hurt themselves over petty issues. Seldom do they realize that their way of attitude in itself is a primary cause of their stressful relationships, and that they can make their living more worthwhile by altering their self-conceived notion of perfection.

If you ever happen to get caught into the uncontrollable temperament, as was Chris, and suffer unmanageable stress due to that, I advise you examine your attitude and find ways to alter it.

One way to alter such attitude is mental affirmation in meditation. I once offered Chris a tip. He took it seriously. He would come a little early to work and stay in his car for a few minutes before beginning his work. During this brief period, he would repeat a small affirmation of the nature that would encourage him to accept his workplace just the way it was.

I had further asked him to close his eyes and hold his focus between his eyes when exercising the affirmation. He used to repeat it earnestly for some five times. His attitude of perfection seemed to be mellowing down. It became more acceptable. I have discussed about this technique of affirmation in Chapter Seven and elsewhere in this book. Nevertheless, I have offered below a couple of tips and some sample affirmations, hoping they may come handy to you, if ever needed.

While leaving home to meet your life's daily challenges you may affirm to yourself: "I shall play whatever roles, my life may offer me today, to the best of my abilities, and shall not be unduly concerned over their outcome." "I will strive for the best, and will not invite what I do not like by unduly worrying about them." "If I happen to work again with the same unfriendly individual, I shall not lose my professional demeanor no matter what may come." "If the situation turns out contrary to my expectation, I shall try to accept it as gracefully as I can, and try to seek a meaning in it for my growth." You can craft your own affirmation, as Chris did, appropriate to the nature of the challenge at a given moment.

When discovered that stress and suffering in your life are due to your own behavior, you must take the situation more seriously. Examine your attitude more objectively and try to alter yourself from within rather than only your behavior. Our very habits, moods and prominent characteristics in our nature determine the level of our stress and happiness.

The risen level of self-awareness in your meditation will help you strive for excellence in place of seeking perfection, and experience personal fulfillment in place of proving something to others or yourself, knowingly or unknowingly. It will help you free yourself from the undesirable traits in your nature, helping you to take your life little easy and get along with others better; the only way to alleviate stress in our lives. Such philosophical reorientation releases our mental energy, often leashed by our attitude of expecting others to act our way.

(4) "What's not Yours, Let it Go"

You might have observed that as we have grown modernized, we have grown more materialistic. Our pursuits have grown oriented to worldly achievements, power, position and possession, more than our personal growth and being considerate to others. This is true in a sense. However, I see differently. There is nothing wrong with possessing as much as we can, and soaring, as high as we can, in the sky of material achievements to take pride and delight in them. After all, it is the very nature of our mind to rise, expand and attain more always.

Our level of happiness depends not on how much we possess, but how we use it. The final objective of all our worldly pursuits, and material possession should be for our personal growth and reaching out to others, and not for simply multiplying it with no noble values attached to them. This narrow perception eventually makes our life simply stressful and miserable. It should rather encourage us to rise above our physical consciousness, and make us think more about our life's purpose.

What we materially possess may become a source of our growth and joy, or the same may become a cause of our stress and pains depending on how we use it. Our imprudent attachment to our possessions may originate stress and the stress related ailments, and contrarily, the use of it with awareness may help enhance our human essence and transform our lives.

Stress comes in life when we develop a sense of possessing it rather than being into it. We do not possess time; we are into it at any given moment. Similarly, it goes with space and life. We do not possess life; we are in fact into it every moment throughout our lives. You might have heard this quote, **"Our life is God's gift to us. What we make out it is our gift to God."** Life is something to live into and experience it. When we perceive our life as our possession like our body, house and bank balance, we fail to understand our life and its subtleties; we fail to recognize the needs of its different realms, and manage it as a whole. This creates chaos and stress. It is like we own a house, but not a home, which we must make to happily live in it.

Remember that everything is subject to the same nature that its source is made of. What we attain from this material world is subject to the nature of its source, impermanence. It is eventually going to return to where it came from. Use what you earn and own for the causes you think right, and do not worry about those things thereafter. Let their life take their own course with the new relationship. **We need to be careful only until we set the aim; once the bullet is released, simply watch and accept the outcome.**

My message is only to remind you not to get possessed by your possessions. Do not get attached to what you possess to an extent that when you lose it, even all of it, you do see it as the end of your life. Whatever is yours you will never lose. You may like the following quote. When visiting a friend's place, I saw a note on their refrigerator, stuck by a small magnet. **"There is nothing free in life. What is yours will be yours even if the whole world tries to snatch it away from you. What is not yours won't make you happy even if it stays with you."**

When involved in a fender-bender accident, do not lose sleep over it for nights. Even a slight dent in your new automobile or house must not make you restless for days. If your flight delays or cancels, and you miss an important meeting, let it go. If you fail to close a lucrative deal, let it go. In spite of giving your best to your work you lose your job, let it go. If you lose your money in the stock markets, let it go. If your house is destroyed by nature's catastrophe or accident, let it go. If a significant relationship in your life breaks despite your best caring for it, let it go.

Do all your best to get it back, to get it repaired, and fight for your rights all the way. Train your mind eventually to let go of things and relationships that you cannot retain or regain despite all your efforts, and seek purpose and solace even in your loss. This is the only way to retain sanity of mind. Think that it served the purpose that it had come with in your life. **Try your best to save and preserve what you love in things and relationships, but if they must go, let them go. Maybe, it was not meant to be yours forever.** Maybe, its relationship with you was over. Maybe, it had to go to make room for some better things in your life.

Change yourself as Chris did in an illustration mentioned earlier. Do not allow any situation, no matter how compelling, to overshadow your peaceful state of mind. Your life is far more than the drama of worldly gains and losses. After taking all measures and precautions, if the outcome turns out to be contrary to your expectations at all, do not feel angry, agonized or frustrated. If this message seems to be making sense to you, touching your inner core, and opening your eyes to a different perception of your life, I am happy to admit that it is my regular practice of meditation that has changed the angle of my perception to the world and its events.

Meditation is a process of gradually heightening our awareness beyond the domains of our mind, which enables us to take our life as a whole, accommodating within it all experiences, pleasant and unpleasant alike, as the integral parts of our life. This comprehensive perception of our life rejects nothing; it accepts each experience and finds in it some meaning for its personal enrichment. It is our very perception that determines our level of happiness and miseries. **Victor Frankl** writes in his *Search For The Meaning In Life*, "Strife cause stress, acceptance transcends it." Changing our belief system is the only way to cure to the increasing stress, and grow immune to its unhealthy influences in our lives. Meditation helps promote such belief system.

(5) *Spiritual Evolution: Our Soul's Ultimate Quest*

As I have quoted earlier, when all human wants, needs and desires are boiled down to a minimum, we are left with only two longings. One is to have someone to talk to, and the other is to have a purpose to welcome tomorrow. One is the longing of our mind, and the other is the quest of our soul. We focus here on discovering the ultimate purpose of our life's journey, and how meditation may help find it and enhance our journey.

The lives of great ones suggest that when we accept the supremacy of our mind over our body, and that of our soul over our mind, our life's purpose becomes clearer to us. The scriptures pronounce that the ultimate purpose of human life is the realization of its highest personal transformation. Our soul needs a physical body for mobility and interactions with our outside world, and mind to gather experiences for its spiritual journey. Thus we see that our mind is a bridge between its physical counterpart at one end, and its spiritual counterpart at the other. We should therefore train our mind to gather and delve into only those experiences, which may continually nourish our soul's needs and speed its journey.

Saints and wise people pronounce that an ideal way of living is to stay engaged in meeting our worldly duties with awareness, and yet stay focused on the ultimate purpose of life's journey. When not aware of the purpose of our life's journey, we neglect our spiritual needs, the highest among all faculties, creating a disorder, and sometimes chaos in our daily priorities.

Meditation, as you know by now, promotes our attitude and transforms our perception of the events in our lives. Though still fighting life's battles as before, we respond to them now with a different level of interest. Life's usual problems and priorities do not baffle or frighten us now as before. The hurts, insults and failures do not cause us pains as much as before; we accept them as a passing show of our lives. We draw a message out of the unpleasant encounters for our personal growth, and never think of them again. Meditation helps develop such a state of our mental attitude.

Nevertheless, meditation is not the only way to

nurture our soul's needs and help realize the mental attitude described above. There are other ways, too. Prayer, fellowship with the saints, and scriptural study are the other ways that I have found equally beneficial in my practicing them. Nevertheless, our prayers often tend to be more of a petition compared to an unconditional surrender, and such saints who are truly advanced on the path that we aspire to follow are seldom to be found, and furthermore, difficult to be recognized by our ill trained minds.

Between the remainder of the other ways, meditation brings to us a direct realization of the truth, compared to the scriptures, which come down to us through several layers of human interpretations and are mostly written in a cryptic language. Therefore, in my personal practice, I have experienced that meditation is more effective, and have accepted the scriptural studies as supplementary. In the deep recesses of our meditative silence, we connect ourselves to the deepest core of our being, the nature of which is spiritual.

Once we begin realizing the presence of our spiritual consciousness, even if just momentarily, our whole perception toward our world and life transforms. This realization however immensely fortifies our natural immunity. Once we rise above the influences of our critical mind, we naturally rise above all negative influences of the stresses in our lives.

If you study the lives of the wise people and spiritual masters, what one thing, common to them, may amaze you is this: Despite the fact that they suffer trials and tribulations in their lives, often far more than the most of us, they hardly experience the stress as we do in our daily lives. Though seemingly no different than us, they possess a different level of responsive attitude to the encounters in their lives. This is what distinguishes them from us. This is the power of meditation, to raise our consciousness to a higher plateau, increasing our natural immunity against the stressful influences in our lives.

Summary

In this chapter, you have studied the five benefits of meditation in our spiritual realm, which I have personally experienced in varying degrees. They are: (1) A Loyal Companion Discovered, (2) Middle-Age Crisis, (3) Seeking Perfection Is Not Always A Virtue, (4) "What is not yours let it go," and (5) Spiritual Evolution: Our Soul's Ultimate Quest.

Our life is like a square, its physical, mental and emotional faculties forming its three sides, and our spiritual faculty its base. Once we recognize our life as a square, made of four faculties, each possessing its own individuality, and yet, depending on others for its sustenance and growth, our perception of life transforms. We begin understanding the subtleties of our life better. I remind you therefore not to ignore the needs of each of these faculties, especially of your spiritual one, which is the foundation of all. This we may be able to accomplish by the four ways discussed in this chapter.

The two primary causes of overall stress in our lives are: one, our failure to respond to the needs of our life's different faculties, and two, not being able to timely identify the disharmony, if any, between the faculties. Discovering the purpose of our life's journey helps us to place our daily priorities in a right perspective, liberating us from the impacts of the mounting stress in our daily life.

- - - - - - - - - -

Highlights of
Benefits At Our Spiritual Level

(1)   When narrowed to a minimum of all our needs, wants
        and desires, what we have are two longings in our
        lives: Having someone to talk to, a discovering the
        purpose to live for. All causes of stress in different areas
        of our lives originate from our not being able to
        identify these longings of our lives. Once you begin
        meditating sincerely, this realization begins unfolding
        to you naturally.

(2)   A perpetual state of peace and self-composure is
        attained in life only when we have discovered a loyal,
        trusting friend and the purpose of our life. The wise
        and spiritually oriented people have realized this in
        their voluntary solitude, and so will you too, in your
        regular meditation.

(3)   Any kind of attitudes that hampers us in getting along
        with others, especially in our personal relationships,
        must be altered as soon as possible. Adaptability is a
        virtue. Know that the direct cause of our mental
        restlessness is our very attitude, and again, the same
        attitude, when correctly altered, transforms our life.

(4)   To know and enjoy the best of life, your mental
        attitude needs to be two-pronged. Occasionally,
        distance yourself from your life to observe and
        examine it, and also be into it like the child in his
        play. Such a sense of discrimination develops
        naturally as your meditative practice deepens.

(5)   Habitually seeking perfection in ourselves, and high
        expectations from others is an unhealthy mental
        condition, which often proves futile. Practicing
        meditation, particularly on an affirmation, will enable
        you to reexamine and reprogram your mind just as
        Chris demonstrated, seeking excellence in place of
        perfection.

(6)   It is the very nature of our mind to rise, grow, expand and attain more tirelessly. However, attaching values to your pursuits and achievements will lead you along your life's journey faster than otherwise.

(7)   No matter how preoccupied with your material pursuits, so long you are aware that they are only transitory by nature and instrumental to your higher growth you are in right direction of your progress. This sense of self-awareness, when further developed, will free you from the negative impacts of stress in your life.

(8)   Altering our belief system is the only way to healing the psychological damages caused by our chronic stressful living in the past, and fortifying our immunity against the rising stress in the present. It will bring you the Power of Acceptance over what is unchangeable. **Victor Frankl** writes in *Search For The Meaning In Life*, "Strife causes stress, acceptance transcends it."

(9)   Among the four ways shown to help you discover your life's purpose and meet it,Meditation, prayers, fellowship with saints and scriptural studies, I have found meditation easier to practice and quicker in rewards. Discover the one that suites you the best, and adhere to it with sincerity to enjoy your life to the fullest.

(10) Loneliness is a tragic state of our life. Compared to the actual suffering, the situation of not having some dear one to talk to is even more unbearable as young Cheryl realized. Meditation can alleviate such a condition in our lives. In meditation, the occasional inner experiences of the voice, candlelight, sounds of chimes and gong bells, descending dove, etc., will convince you of the presence of 'someone' within you, like a wise, trusting, ever present companion.

= = = = = = = =

CONCLUSION:

It seems that our entire life is just a play of our mind. The nature and level of our reaction when threatened by a situation largely depends on the nature of the experiences and training that our mind has received up until the present. Basic Psychology discusses the theory of the **stimulus and response**. The situation presented to us is a *stimulus* and our mind's reaction to it is a *response*. The nature of our reaction in the form of a pleasure or pain depends on several factors combined such as our education, parental training, lessons learned from past experiences, and our own personal belief system developed. This is why we find different people reacting differently to the same situation. For example, in a common scenario of congested road traffic or the cancellations of a flight, let alone two strangers, even the twins born and reared by the same biological parents would respond differently.

Well, you may argue, for instance, "Is it not true that when a fire breaks out in a house, all those who are present at that moment are going to demonstrate the same response, and that is, running out for their lives? My answer would be, "No." I say this for the following reason. No two individuals ever act alike although the nature of the challenge is the same. In our scenario, although all those present in the house are seized by the same emotion, panic, and by the same dominant thought of saving their own lives, we may find them reacting still differently.

One person may search for the nearest exit to dash out or a window to jump through, while another person on the run may still try to reach for his cell phone to summon for emergency help for those left behind. One may selfishly grab his personal valuables, and the other may pick up a child, disabled or an elderly person along his way out. One shocked by the fright may drop to the floor, while someone else may first let the women and children escape before himself. Each human is unique and carries within themselves a unique package of prenatal experiences, mental proclivities, emotional maturity, level of philosophical awareness, etc.

Allow me to present another scenario of a similar nature where all concerned individuals experienced the same stimulus and yet, responded in amazingly different ways. It is about the slaves on a US ship. A fire broke out in the boiler room of the ship while it was sailing on high waters. When it became obvious that the fire was uncontrollable, the slaves were released to save their lives. The released slaves demonstrated three kinds of responses to the same situation though identical: (a) Trying to save their own lives, (b) Killing the American soldiers on the ship, or (c) Helping to save the lives of their enemies even at the expense of their own.

One of the slaves saved the lives of nine American soldiers before throwing himself into the sea when he could not bear his burns anymore. Though there were only few such incidents of brave and noble acts among some seventy slaves, it is enough to conclude that it is all up to us how we respond to a situation. We can see that our response depends on the level of our inner attitude and the nature of values that we regard.

Similarly, the causes of stress may be personal such as being overweight, the adverse effects of medications, marital separation, a death in the family, overwork and unhealthy habits. Or they may be environmental in nature such as bad weather, noise pollution and nature's calamities over which we may have little or no control at all. We observed that the effects of stress vary from person to person because each is unique in his upbringing and mental attitude. A crisis to one person may be a challenge to another, and an opportunity to still another. What is quite stressful to you today may not be so stressful to you five years later from now, and the same might be viewed as simply a passing show after few more years.

All these arguments suggest that **the impact of stress depends upon one's level of perception and the sense of acceptability developed.** By nature, stress is subjective and time-sensitive. The more we train ourselves to objectively examine the experiences we encounter, and absorb a deeper meaning than before, the more we grow self-composed. The more we grow self-composed, the better we demonstrate clarity in our thinking and prudence in judgments. This heightened level of self-awareness transforms our attitude towards our life's battles, enabling us to rise above the impact of increasing negative stresses in our day-to-day life. **The act of daily self-reflection is one of the simplest ways to understand and rise above the increasing stress in our daily life.**

Another way to rise above the influences of negative stress is to recognize the needs of each of our four faculties—physical, mental, emotional and spiritual—and their interdependence. Sound health and fulfilling biological needs form our physical faculty. Striving to meet the worldly pursuits, professional achievements and life's desires comprise our mental faculty. Healthy and genuine relationships nurture our emotional faculty.

And finally, attributing higher values to all our material achievements and worldly pursuits, playing prudently the diverse roles of our lives, and pondering over the purpose of our sojourn, nurtures the needs of our spiritual faculty, the most often neglected aspect of ourselves. Focusing on only one side of our nature such as the mental faculty, and ignoring others creates disharmony within us. It is like a family divided within that can never be at peace and in its full strength

I have sometimes used the words 'spiritual' and 'philosophical' interchangeably only in a light manner. At a deeper level, they suggest different connotations. To me, spirituality deals directly with our soul's evolution, whereas philosophical thinking deals with our intuitive faculty, a state where one is able to distinguish between right and wrong and demonstrate a heightened sense of awareness. Developing our philosophical perception paves a path for our spiritual journey.

All behavioral modifications bring about changes only temporarily. What is needed for a lasting improvement is an attitudinal change from within. The focus of conventional medical practice tends to be suppressing the symptoms, rather than identifying their causes, which can originate outside the physical aspect of the individual. A recurrent abdominal pain, steady loss of weight or increasing agitation in mental disposition may have its root in the patient's emotional stress at work, in a personal relationship, or in failing to discover the answers to some metaphysical enigmas, which lie beyond the scope of medical science.

To alleviate stress in life, doctors may recommend changing a job, career or lifestyle, practicing some relaxation method, finding someone to talk to, developing adaptability or changing mental attitudes towards life. However, doctors do not show how to attain it. The scope of medical science, like any other field of specialty, has its own strengths as well as limitations, and its practitioners endeavor to adhere to the books of their field of knowledge.

This reminds me one of **Schwadron's** cartoon strips wherein a physician is shown finally admitting to his patient: **"You need some human caring and a reassuring touch, but I am afraid that was not a part of my medical curriculum."** Limitations of the conventional medical treatments are obvious and we must accept them. We need to realize that our life is not only the body that we see, and the mind that provides it a power of mobility and sensuous pleasures, but two other faculties as well, the emotional and spiritual, and that all aspects are interrelated, making our life one whole unit.

I believe, therefore, that in order to take charge of our life, rather than simply depending on external aids such as painkillers and anti-depressants, we must discover ways to fortify our natural immunity. One of the ways that I have experienced in my own life and have found highly effective is turning within. This may enable us to awaken our mind's often unrecognized and underused powers, and alter our belief system. **Daily meditation, prayers, self-introspection, scriptural reading, and fellowship of wise people are also equally powerful ways to develop our natural immunity.**

For every problem in our health, there is a special branch of study, and its experts are relentlessly engaged in researching more ways to improve the quality of human life. For instance, physicians are engaged with treating our physical illnesses, psychiatrists with mental disorders; psychologists with human behavior, and clergies and theologians with our souls and spiritual healing. And yet, we find ourselves helpless when time comes seeking ways to live a balanced life, or dealing with hostile encounters calmly, or finding answers of our life's enigmas. This reality in our lives reminds us to keep exploring means to take better charge of our life. If you choose meditation as a discipline to understand your life better and take charge of it as I did, and many of those who I came into contact with, I have no doubt that reading this book again will help you guide step by step in your practice, and forewarn you against the obstacles that I had to face.

Those with a heightened sense of self-awareness understand their health better and can catch an imbalance in their health before it grows into a serious problem. The more we are aware of the changes in ourselves, the more we shall develop independence to medications and personal suffering. **Meditation transforms our perception, heightens our self-awareness and enhances our level of endurance.** Practice any method of meditation that may best suit your mental tendencies and life style.

We have discussed four methods of meditation each of which is varying only in its focus—breathing, music, thoughts and *mantra* or affirmation. The ultimate objective of each is the same: Your mental relaxation, gradually helping you realize your inner power and developing a sense of personal indifference to factors unmanageable factors of life. Remember that certain events in our lives are unpredictable and when they strike us they bring upon us devastating effects. These events might be an incurable disease, marital separation, loss of a long employment or life-long earning, and a death of our beloved. Such events break down average people, but not those who sincerely practice meditation or some similar discipline.

Devote a little time everyday to voluntarily withdraw your mind from outside world to your inner world. Sit about twenty minutes quietly or listening to such music that may stir you within and helps transcend your material awareness. A wholehearted prayer of self-surrender is also a mode of meditation. The whole objective of secluding inwardly is to take away your thoughts from the worldly objects and relationships for a few minutes, like a turtle withdrawing itself under its hard shell for self-protection. There should be no excuse for not having that little time at the end of the day for something that promises our optimal growth.

As much as healthy food and a good night's sleep is essential to our body, so is a regular practice of mind transcending itself from its incessant thought processes, the only way to make our mind sharper in clarity and creativity. A composed state of mind engenders noble thoughts and prudent decisions. I suggest that you **continue playing at your best the different roles at a given time in your life, which could be as a parent, child, spouse, employer or employee, and yet stay unattached to its outcome. The examples given of a lotus, emergency room physicians and 911-attendants should encourage you exemplify this message.**

Enjoy every moment when in the world, and yet learn to withdraw yourself from it for a little while everyday. I shared with you how I could manage to stay self-composed for months when I had to work with an unfriendly team leader. Try to develop such a mental attitude as I could, better if you can, focused to your purpose, and yet, nonchalant to other's hostile behavior. Act as prudently as you can, and yet, without showing over concern to its outcome.

A stressed mind obscures our abilities of reasoning and judgment. That is why, though seemingly making decisions meticulously in all realms of our lives such as health, careers, relationships, and financial investment, we often seem to be failing in making a desired progress. If meditation seems to be failing to bring the desired benefits in your life, I may remind you, as I did to Paul (Chapter 8), to reinforce your practice with the Powers of Reminder, Environment and Visualization.

These three power-tools can be employed to any discipline in your life, including weight loss, rebuilding a relationship, worldly accomplishments, and making more money for faster progress. Taking the aid of the power-tools during the beginning of your discipline will certainly encourage you to stay focused where most are often found disappointed.

Knowing the benefits of meditation, simple in practice and enormously effective in personal growth, I highly advocate that a discipline of this nature should be introduced at an early age to our young adults, tomorrow's corporate and national leaders, who will be challenged to make the right decisions at every step in their careers. The more the young adults, in homes and schools, are oriented to a practice of sitting quietly with an inward focus for a few minutes, the more they will mature in making prudent decisions for themselves as well as others.

Playing a leadership role well primarily requires an independent thinking and a self-composed mind; the decisions made otherwise often invite disgrace and downfall.

The effectiveness of the conventional leadership programs offered at university level and corporate workshops depends mainly on the nature of the training received by the young leaders during their early years in homes and schools. The age period of 14 through 20 years is normally the determining period in one's life for the level of growth and success in one's future.

I suggest that schools may periodically invite experts in this field to speak, teach and demonstrate how meditation can be practiced. A curriculum in schools and colleges could consist of a course on living a balanced life, which may prove equally helpful, like the other subjects offered, such as philosophy, religious studies and environmental science, helping thus our young generation to grow into responsible citizens and better human beings. The topics in these programs may focus on the ways and benefits of inward silence, uniform breathing, effectively playing different roles as siblings, students, neighbors, community members and citizens.

The young adults may not fully realize the values of the discipline they will receive now, but they will recognize someday how Hitler and Abraham Lincoln were different though both were acclaimed as the most successful world leaders in their own ways. **This will enable them to awaken the little Lincoln, and be careful about the little Hitler in them.**

The earlier the young adults are encouraged to realize the discriminatory sense, the earlier they will be able to distinguish between the right and wrong; and the earlier they are encouraged to develop a sense of self-awareness, the earlier they will begin developing a positive attitude and stand stronger for their convictions and values. As much as they are trained to be successful in the world outside, they also need to be trained to be successful in their personal lives, whereupon rests the key of getting along with others and realizing a true sense of commitment and contentment in life.

Disrespect to peers, parents, teachers and law originate out of not having developed respect for oneself. Respecting others and their properties is only a dimension of our self-respect. On realizing this, the schools and universities will be in a better position to carry on their roles from where the parents may have left.

We have sports and gymnastic trainings in our schools to help students grow sound physically and develop a sense of competitiveness; we have the subjects of science and technologies for their intellectual development; and we have the subjects such as poems, literature, painting and theatrical arts to nurture their emotional faculties and creative longings. It is the same with the training in the realms of meditation, balanced living, self-esteem, positive attitude and philosophical reorientation, which will help them to demonstrate their decisions more judiciously in their careers, relationship and leaderships roles at all levels. It will help them stay positive and self-composed in the difficult times of their lives.

Practicing meditation or a similar method that encourages one to sit mentally withdrawn from the outside world is the only way to achieve these results described above. **The level of material possession, position or social power alone in our lives must not measure the level of our true success.** It must equally include how prudent decisions we are able to make in our personal relationships. As a nation's strength, stability and progress are determined by the characters of her people, a corporation's growth is determined by the level of its employees' morale and its leaders' decision-making abilities. A structured training program of meditation promises forming a sound character, making prudent decisions and embarking greater challenges with more success.

- - - - -

NOTES

REFERENCES & RECOMMENDATIONS

Avalon, Arthur (Sir John Woodroffe), *The SERPENT POWER, The Secrets of Tantric and Shakti Yoga*, Dover Publications, Inc, New York, 1958

Frankl, Victor E., *Man's Search For Meaning, An Introduction to Logotherapy*, paperback edition, Pocket Books, New York, 1985

Janiger, Oscar, M.D. and Goldberg, Phillip, *Different Kind of Healing*, G.P Putnam's Sons, N.Y., 1994

Krishna, Gopi, *KUNDALINI, The Evolutionary Energy in Man*, Shambhala Publications, Inc. Boston, U.S.A., 1971

Pelletier, Kenneth R., *Mind As Healer, Mind As Slayer*, Dell Publishing, 1540 Broadway, New York, N.Y. 10036, 1992.

Yogananda, Paramahansa, *Autobiography Of A Yogi*, Self-Realization Fellowship, Los Angeles, CA 90065, 1971

_____, *The Bhagvad Gita, Royal Science of God-Realization*, Self- Realization Fellowship, Los Angeles, CA 90065, 1995.

_____, *The Divine Romance*, Self- Realization Fellowship, Los Angeles, CA 90065, 1986.

_____, *Journey To Self-Realization*, Self- Realization Fellowship, Los Angeles, CA 90065, Reprint 2000.

_____, *Man's Eternal Quest*, Self- Realization Fellowship, Los Angeles, CA 90065, 1985.

MEDITATION

The *10* Power Tips for Faster Benefits

1   Practice with a receptive attitude.

2   Practice in solitude, away from distractions.

3   Sit straight and comfortably with your feet resting on the ground or a footstool.

4   Remain seated a while, and open your eyes slowly, after your practice ends.

5   Practice regularly, at the same place and time, for faster results.

6   Persist to practice even when you feel tired and restless.

7   Practicing soon after a heavy meal is not recommended.

8   Share your sacred experiences with the like-minded individuals only.

9   Do not be discouraged when your mind fails to experience peace even after the days of your practice. Self-transformational discipline needs sometimes more patience.

10 Join a meditation group occasionally for a change and motivation.

SUMMARY OF QUOTES

"All man's miseries derive from his not being able to sit quietly in a room alone."

(Blaisal Pascal)

"We have learned how to make a living, but not a life; added years to our life, but not life to our years."

(George Carlin)

"Meditation is the science of God-realization."

(Paramahansa Yogananda)

"When you pray, enter into your closet...and your Father who sees in secret shall reward you openly."

(Matthew 6:6)

"You rise as high as the influence of a person of your inspiration."

(Paramahansa Yogananda)

"Learn to be silent, Let your quiet mind listen and absorb."

(Pythagoras)

"To go very far, you must begin very near and near is you, the 'you' that you must understand."

(J. Krishnamurti)

"...Kundalini (The source of psychic energies), is the real cause of all genuine spiritual and psychic phenomena, the biological basis of evolution and development of personality...."

(Gopi Krishna)

"Seek and you will find, ask and you will receive, knock and it will open."

(The Bible)

"The right music is the one that stirs you within and transcends your senses."

(Arun "Yogi" Parekh)

"With our thoughts we make our future,
with our thoughts we change our world."

(The Buddha)

"You know what you are, but you do not know what you may be."

(Shakespeare)

"The greatest discovery of my generation is that human beings can alter their lives by altering their attitudes."

(William James)

"Do not do what you want,
and then you may do what you like."

(Swami Sadashiv)

"Those who cannot get along with themselves
cannot get along with others."

(Paramahansa Yogananda)

"The greatest discovery of my generation is that human beings, by changing the inner attitude of their minds, can change the outer aspects of their lives."

(William James)

"We have multiplied our possessions but reduced our values. We talk of love but keep it limited to making love only. We visit church more but bring god in life less. We have learned how to make a living, but not a life. We have added years to ourlife but not life to our years."

(George Carlin)

"The mind . . . in itself can make a heaven of hell and hell of heaven."

(John Milton)

"Be very careful with what you set your heart upon, for you will surely have it."

(Ralph Waldo Emerson)

"Meditation is an effort in the beginning. Later on it becomes habitual and gives bliss, joy and peace."

(Swami Sivananda)

"What lies behind us and what lies before usare tiny matters compared to what lies within us."

(Ralph Waldo Emerson)

"Our life is God's gift to us. What we make of it is our gift to God."

(Anon)

"There is nothing free in life. What is yours will be yours even if the whole world tries to snatch it away from you. What is not yours won't make you happy even if it stays with you."

(Anon)

"Strife cause stress, acceptance transcends it."

(Victor Frankl)

Maharshi Mahesh Yogi: If meditation is practiced by even one percent of the population of America, it would generate a positive change in the overall thinking of the entire nation.

Paramahansa Yogananda: "Our mind is like a crystal, which has a natural tendency to pick up the shape and color of the object nearest it."

Paramahansa Yogananda: "Struggling to maintain a certain physical posture is not essential for meditation, but it certainly accelerates the effect. A bent posture is dangerous to the spine because it may throw its discs or vertebrae off their alignment."

Ralph Waldo Emerson in his *Compensation:*
"The world looks like a mathematical equation, which turn anyhow you will, balances itself. Every secret is told, every crime is punished, every virtue is rewarded, and every wrong is redressed, in silence and certainty."

Eleanor Roosevelt: "No one can insult you unless you accept it."

Mahatma Gandhi is quoted to say this:

Watch your thoughts, because
  your thoughts will become your words;
Watch your words, because
  your words will become your actions;
Watch your actions, because
  your actions will become your habits;
Watch your habits, because
  your habits will become your attitude;
Watch your attitude, because
  your attitude will become your values;
Watch your values, because
  your values will become your character;
Watch your character, because
  your character will make your destiny.

An Eastern saying: "For one to be little others, the one has to be little first."

Hitler: "A lie when repeated a thousand times, becomes a truth in itself."

We Help Achieve Human Potential

We believe that we possess countless possibilities in our lives, but we are not fully aware of them. To succeed further and stay focused, we need at times someone to remind us that "Yes, we can do it." Our presentations will help your employees, at all levels, to recognize the infinite potentials they possess, and our programs showing them the ways to realize them. A lasting growth occurs in our lives only when we realize the need of a change, and the necessary changes are made from within rather than making only behavioral changes.

We Offer

+ Guided Meditation
+ Stress Management
+ Positive Attitude
+ Meeting Higher Goals
+ Retiring Happily

We Present

+ Keynotes
+ Training
+ Workshops
+ Seminars

We Present To

+ Community leader
+ Corporate Executieves
+ Youth Groups
+ Retirees
+ Survivors of
  Traumas & Tragediies

+ Corporations
+ Conferences
+ Conventions
+ Associations
+ Spiritual Retreats
+ University Campuses
+ Rehabilitation Centers

Our programs, drawn on timeless teachings and personal convictions, will enhance the values, productivity and morale at all levels of your employees.

Arun"Yogi" Parekh, M.A.
(Speaker & Trainer)

Our Approach:
Direct and Practical

- - - - - - - - - - - - - - - - - - -

We *teach how to make homes,*
more than making houses.

We *teach how to make a life,*
more than making a living.

We *teach how to add life to our years,*
more than adding years to our life.

We *teach how to connect,*
more than communicating.

We *teach how to seek values in goals,*
more than only meeting goals.

We *talk of no personal gods,*
but of discovering our conscience.

We *talk of no individual faiths,*
but of seeking the meaning of rituals.

We *talk of no spirituality,*
but of developing perception of life.

We *talk of no heaven and hell,*
but of playing well our diverse roles.

Arti Integrated Training www.ArtiPresentations.com

OUR PROGRAM OVERVIEW

MEDITATION

✦ It trains our mind to detach itself from our thoughts and feelings for few minutes daily to help them grow healthier.

✦ Relaxed mind enables us know ourselves at a deeper level and realize many possibilities of our lives.

✦ The deeper we dive inwardly, the more we achieve outwardly.

✦ Meditation centers us, grounds us, and enables us to deal with the world with more poise and strength.

✦ Meditation helps us think clearly, judge prudently and invite in our lives honest relationships.

STRESS MANAGEMENT

✦ A composed mind better helps us to make decisions, organize our priorities and play our diverse roles enabling us thus to control over the three common causes of our stress.

✦ Tuning in with our inner silence heightens our philosophical perception, a lasting remedy of our stressful living.

✦ A daily practice of withdrawing ourselves briefly from our lives' countless demands draws our body, mind, heart and soul in a closer harmony. Self-composure is our power over all negative powers.

POSITIVE ATTITUDE

✦ An attitude is the sum total of influences absorbed by our mind combined by its prenatal experiences.

✦ A child's quality of life is almost determined at the time of his or her conception by the parents' thoughts prevalent then.

✦ Our life is shaped more by our attitude and faith in ourselves than the forces around us.

✦ Those who leave marks behind possess one thing in common, often uncommon to the masses, a firm faith in their sustained positive attitude.

MEETING HIGHER GOALS

✦ Goals fill our minds with pride and our lives with worldly success. But Higher Goals bring a purpose and lasting fulfillment to our lives.

✦ Higher Goals aim at attributing noble values to our worldly goals.

✦ Higher Goals help us realize that the power, position and possession in our lives are only the means to make us humbler and nobler.

✦ Higher Goals help us discover one day our life's dream. Mahatma Gandhi had such a dream: "I want to see my India free." So had Martin Luther King Jr. and Thomas Edison.

NOTES

NOTES